Xing Yi
She Xing

Xing Yi
She Xing

SVP

Published by S.V.P

Copyright © S.V.P 2023

The moral right of S.V.P to be identified as the author of this work has been asserted. All rights reserved. No part of this book may be reproduced in any form or by any means without prior permission in writing from the publisher.

ISBN 978-1-7392934-0-6

Note:

The author and publisher do not accept any responsibility or liability for loss, injury or damage arising from the use or misuse of any of the information contained in this book.

Photography Credits:

Emma Heeney for the main photography throughout this book.

Mike Ash - pages 107, 113

Pravin Bagde on Unsplash - page 19, Museums Victoria on Unsplash - page 26, David Clode on Unsplash - page 47, Alfonso Castro on Unsplash - page 51, Laura Barry on Unsplash - page 54, Jan Kubita on Unsplash - page 66, Vikas Shankarathota on Unsplash - page 68.

*This book is dedicated to my Xing Yi teacher,
Damon Smith*

國立故宮博物院藏品

形意拳

Acknowledgements

I would first like to thank my friend and teacher Damon Smith. For the ongoing instruction, advice and support over the many years that we have known each other.

A big thank you to my friend Graham Barlow, firstly for introducing me to Damon all of those years ago at the infamous Wick training ground, and also for kindly writing his article in the appendix.

To Mike Ash for the years of training, friendship and for some of the photographs in this book.

A big thank you to Emma Heeney for her excellent photographic skills.

To Sifu Raymond Rand, Sifu Donald Kerr, Sifu Doug Robertson, and all of the other amazing people in the Yongquan Martial Arts Association. Also to Derek Williams and Brett Galloway.

Finally, I would like to thank the National Palace Museum in Taipei, for kindly allowing me to use a number of their images of Song Dynasty artwork.

Contents

Initial Words *(Sifu Raymond Rand)* — page X
Foreword *(Sifu Damon Smith)* — page XI
Introduction by the Author — page XIV

Xing Yi's Twelve Animals (Shi Er Xing) — page 1

Xing Yi Snake (She Xing) — page 13

Yang Snake (Yang She Xing) — page 27

Yin Snake (Yin She Xing) — page 35

She Xing Applications — page 43

Lian Huan – Linking Sequence — page 76

A She Xing Linking Sequence — page 78

She Xing Weapons: Wu-Bing Fa — page 83

Contents

Appendix

- Contents — page 92
- The Shenfa (Body Methods) — page 93
- The Eight Jins of Xing Yi — page 96
- The Seven Stars — page 101
- Dark and Bright Jin Striking — page 102
- Our Xing Yi Lineage — page 104
- Other Books in this Series and Info on Xing Yi Groups in the UK — page 105
- San Ti Shi (Three Body Posture) — page 108
- A Comparison of Xing Yi Snake and BJJ, by Graham Barlow — page 114

About the Author — page 128

Glossary of Xing Yi terminology — page 130

Initial Words

Snakes, like spiders, aren't everyone's cup of tea. It's often the motion of these predatory species that upsets people with an aversion to their appearance but, certainly in the case of the snake, it's the way in which the animal moves which generates its power.

Snakes are phenomenally successful predators. Many modern snake groups originated during the Paleocene period (66 to 55 million years ago) and have been exploiting their ecological niche ever since. There is much to be learned from this evolutionary masterpiece, for those interested in developing their understanding of Xing Yi or martial arts in general.

In the art of Xing Yi two types of snake are studied: the Viper and the Boa Constrictor. Vipers represent the Yang aspect of snake strategy, Boa Constrictors the Yin.

In this book the author methodically introduces both aspects of snake form (She Xin), beginning with the Viper and progressing to the Boa Constrictor. Examining both the form of the snake's movement and also the intent, which together become the strategy of these reptilian super predators.

I have known author for several years. He is a student of Sifu Damon Smith and his knowledge of this subject is a testament; both to Sifu Smith's teaching and his own tenacity, hard work and enthusiasm for the training of Xing Yi.

If you study the art of Xing Yi, or simply want to gain an understanding of the snake as an approach to martial arts, this book is a must.

Sifu Raymond Rand
Senior Instructor, Yongquan Martial Arts Association

Foreword

The Snake has played a leading role in the collective consciousness of the Chinese people since antiquity. In order to understand this role, westerners must first put aside the cultural notions of snakes found in our Abrahamic traditions.

In China, the snake was never accursed or forced to crawl on its belly as punishment for ancient wrong but was instead a sublimely adapted animal of rich and varied character.

In premodern China the Snake held powerful symbolism and was an important source of traditional Chinese medicines. Two and a half thousand years ago, Confucius recorded traditional songs and poems involving, among other things, the characters and exploits of snakes in his Shi Ching.

By the time of the Tang Dynasty (618-906AD) an almost scientific study of snakes had begun. For instance, Hsun Liu made observations of the Liang Tou She (*Calamaria septentrionalis*), a snake that was believed at that time to have two heads.

This snake survives today and does indeed appear to have two heads, one at each end of its body. Both heads are extremely similar in appearance and exhibit the same movements and behaviour, striking with equal ferocity at targets that come within range.

However, Hsun Liu noted that the snake always moved in the direction of only one of the heads, and was the first to realise that there was really only one head, the other being a cleverly adapted "fake" head at the end of the tail that serves the purpose of fooling or confusing predators into thinking they are taking on two snakes at once.

Through subsequent generations the detailed study of snakes and other animals in China became increasingly sophisticated. This trend reached its golden age in the work of Shichen Lee (1518-1593), who was active in the generation before Master Ji Long Feng formulated Hsing-I in its current guise.

In his book Ben Tsao Gang Mu, Shichen Lee left us a picture of how animals were viewed by those who, like Ji Long Feng, were interested in learning about and from wild animals during the Ming Dynasty. In particular, he divided the study of animals into five broad subject areas: Chong, Lin, Chai, Ching and Shou. Snakes belonged to the Lin category, as did Tuo (the Hsing-I Alligator or Crocodile).

As a result of the relative notoriety of Shichen Lee and other experts in the later Ming Dynasty, the work of Ji Long Feng, in his creation or re-formulation of Hsing-I as something close to the form in which we have it today, together with his basing the art almost exclusively upon the characters of wild animals (the five elements being added to Hsing-I at a later time), should be viewed in a context in which a relatively high level of interest in animals and the natural world had been sparked among the Chinese population of the time.

Today, despite quite a few man-made extinctions, the Chinese remain truly blessed with the number and variety of snakes that occur in their homeland. In all there are more than 200 species, covering every type of behaviour and trait of the snake family as a whole, including many behaviours and features that the average person would not associate with snakes.

I was very pleased when my student asked me to write the foreword to his book on Snake, as it is a book that I would have liked to have written myself, something that I am never going to have time to actually do.

The author has committed himself to the study of the martial arts for more than 30 years, and has been my personal student for about 17 years. He is a person of great character and dedication, and, together with Graham Barlow who appears in the appendix, is one of a top handful of my Hsing-I students. I do hope you enjoy his book on the fascinating and often surprising subject of Hsing-I Snake.

Sifu Damon Smith, Senior Xing Yi Instructor
Yongquan Martial Arts Association

Introduction by the Author

It has been a several years since I started writing my first book on Xing Yi. When I started to type the first words of that book I never dreamed that it would be as successful as it has been, and I am pleased that many Xing Yi practitioners around the world are getting something out of it.

This has now spurred me on to write the next book in the series and hopefully I will be able to keep the momentum going, so as to complete the rest of the books on Xing Yi's animals over the coming years.

Xing Yi is a vast martial art with incredible depth, which is something that many people fail to realise. There are many who think that they have reached the pinnacle of the art after practicing some Five Elements Xing Yi for a few years. The Five Elements are good for learning some of the basics of the art, before attempting to endeavour on the much harder task of practicing and embodying the Xing Yi animals.

The animals in Xin(g) Yi are where the art lies, and it is true to say that without them you have not really travelled far into the system. Five elements Xing Yi was a later addition to the art, which was most likely added by the Dai family. My gut feeling (and others) is that Master Dai Long Bang added the Five Elements Boxing to his family's Xing Yi syllabus, as a much quicker way to try and teach the art to beginners – if you like, 'an easier door in'.

Trying to teach any of the animals from the outset is very difficult, and this is due to the immense subtlety which is involved with each of the different animal's strategies, methods and ways of creating Jin (warrior force).

Within the animals of this fascinating art, you will find yourself immersed in a challenge which will last your whole lifetime, as you will never stop improving and refining your Xing Yi. Deepening your connection, not only to the animals themselves, but also to the Xin. Making the art one of the most profound and effective systems, which will re-connect you to Nature and your place within it.

I hope that you enjoy this book and get something out of it, which hopefully can be used to improve your own Xing Yi practice. Even if you take one small thing away from reading this study of Xing Yi Snake (She Xing), then I will be happy that it was worth all of the effort that went into writing it.

國立故宮博物院藏品

Xing Yi's Twelve Animals (Shi Er Xing)

'It is a single origin that splits into infinite branches, and these infinite branches all belong to one origin...'

Xing Yi is an art derived from the use of the spear (Qiang), which was tried and tested on the battlefields of China during the feudal era, from the Song dynasty onwards (Song dynasty, 960-1279). Practiced by the elite ranks in the army, Xing Yi (or Yue Fei Quan as it was once known) developed into a fascinating and no-nonsense fighting system which is without doubt, devastatingly effective.

Although the techniques themselves developed from the spear, the art is also a reflection on the vast and unceasing complexity that comes directly from Nature. The Xing Yi masters of old studied the wild animals which they came across, and it was from a select group of these creatures, that they copied and ultimately embodied their characters (Xing), to use to defeat their opponents during combat.

These animals were chosen due to their unique fighting abilities, which had given these creatures huge advantages during their evolution, and which enabled them to thrive and push themselves to the top of the food chain. It can be seen that the original masters of Xing Yi also picked a group of animal characters that were quite different from each other, which is evident in the way in which they hunt, protect themselves and survive.

This variation of animals contained within the Xing Yi syllabus, which we can still see in the modern era, gives the practitioner a huge array of methods and strategies with which to defeat any potential opponent.

Within our school, and indeed most schools of Xing Yi descending from Master Guo Yun Shen, there are Twelve Animals which are formally studied within the syllabus.

It is worth noting though, that there are other animals that have been embodied and whose fighting strategies have been used in combat. I have personally seen and studied some other animals which are not often seen in Xing Yi - these are Crane, Wild Cat and Mandarin Duck. I have also heard that the Lion was an animal Xing which was studied in the past — although not a native creature to China, some Emperors kept them as pets, and therefore people in China had definitely come into contact with them, and obviously had the chance to study their characters.

Starting Out

In our lineage, and the way in which I and others were taught, the Twelve Animals followed a 'loose' pattern which was helpful to the student attempting to learn a particular Xing. Note: In our school this generally follows on from the initial training in the Five Elements, which lays a good foundation in Xing Yi dynamics, stability and power generation.

A good starting place for learning the animals is Bear-Eagle (Xiong Ying), as it contains the most Yin (Bear) and the most Yang (Eagle) aspects of all of the animals in Xing Yi. Although She Xing (Snake) is also a good animal to start off with.

So, you can begin by learning a linking sequence (Lian Huan) for Bear-Eagle and then concentrate on keeping the Bear sections of the link very Yin and the Eagle sections very Yang. This is hard to do at first, but this is the best animal to attempt this with, and it will give you a flavour of Xing Yi's Yin and Yang approaches to attacking in a combat situation. You will need to be able to switch between the Yin and Yang  phases of this strategy seamlessly for it to work properly. So, in some ways it can be said that things are slightly less subtle with Bear-Eagle, and this therefore gives the student a chance to learn their first animal strategy (or two animals if you view the Bear and Eagle as a separate Xing each).

Of course, when practicing linking or 'lian huan' of any animal (or Five Elements) in Xing Yi, you are aiming to embody what is known and termed as 'free-linking' – where you move between the different structures you create in a spontaneous and free manner. But to start to learn an animal it is necessary for the student to be taught a set pattern, so that they have something to latch on to, enabling them to get a feel for the 'flavour' of a particular animal Xing.

It is worthy of noting here that every human being is unique in the way that they move. Their size/weight and of course their own natural strategy, are all dependent on the way in which their mind and intention is being driven. Therefore you will find that each student will naturally gravitate towards one of the animals in the Xing Yi syllabus, as it will suit their preferred way of moving and genetic make-up.

This will normally be obvious to the teacher from the outset but is often not mentioned, as it is more beneficial for the Xing Yi student to practice all of the animals and become a more well-rounded fighter before they realise which strategy (Xing) is best or more suited to them. If you mention this too early in their training then the student may put more effort into that strategy at the detriment of the others, which can make it harder for them to master any other animal Xing in the future.

Moving onto the other Animal Xings (after Bear-Eagle), the water becomes a lot more muddied and unclear, as they don't sit on the extreme ends of the spectrum of Yin and Yang (to varying degrees) – therefore the level of subtlety will be completely lost on someone who is starting out, especially with the advanced Animal Xings within the Xing Yi syllabus. Which is why Bear-Eagle (Xiong Ying) is a great place to start.

In this context we are talking about the Yin aspect as nurturing the situation, and not actively going for the opponent, although the strikes feel very dense and heavy. The Yang aspect is very different and actively goes out to meet the opponent, while setting up/advancing the attack; the strikes are obviously still heavy.

An Jin Striking

As our school is from a lineage descending from Grand Masters Li Neng Ran and Guo Yun Shen, it prefers to produce and use Dark Jin (An Jin) when delivering any of these strikes, whether they are derived from a Yin or Yang strategy. Jin in this context can be translated as 'warrior force' and Dark Jin has a very heavy and dense feel to it. When striking with Dark Jin the opponent's body is displaced as the strike passes straight through their previous position, which is akin to an eagle taking its prey, where the eagle's talons and body will pass through its target's position. Needless to say, this is a skill which is well worth the time required to learn it. When you have a feel for, and are able to produce this type of striking, it delivers a serious 'shock factor' to your opponent who may not have been struck in such a heavy, piercing and displacing manner before.

Historically, An Jin striking was developed and favoured by practitioners of the art who were adept in the use of the Spear (Qiang) – this allowed the point of the weapon to pass through the armour of an opponent much more easily. Of course, the same concept applies to any weapon which the practitioner happens to be using, ensuring that the strike passes into and through the opponent as far as possible to cause maximum damage.

The other broad category of striking which is used in Xing Yi is termed Bright Jin (Ming Jin) where the energy is borrowed in a number of ways to create a whiplash effect that shakes the insides of the opponent. Although we favour the An Jin striking within the Hebei branches of the art descending from Masters Guo and Li, we also practice Ming Jin striking and some of the animal strategies depend upon this type of energy production for success. Yang She Xing, or Yang Snake being one of these animals.

It is also worth noting that depending on where you are striking your opponent, you may decide to use either Dark or Bright Jin for a particular result. For example, using Bright Jin strikes to the opponent's head is more effective in knocking them out.

It is important for the Xing Yi practitioner to view both An Jin and Ming Jin as two broad categories for creating striking power, and not to view one as better than the other. Both have their application in Xing Yi, and it is just that the different lineages of the art may prefer to use one way of striking over the other.

Under these two broad categories, all schools of Xing Yi will use the same principles and produce the other eight main Jins, which are Pi, Tsuan, Beng, Fan, Kou, Shun, Heng and Nian Jin.

As our school of Xing Yi has been handed down to us via three different lineages, all descending from Master Guo Yun Shen, it favours An Jin striking. This is because Master Guo was a very successful bodyguard who used an array of weapons to protect pack trains which he would escort across China with his teacher and 'work' colleague Master Li Neng Ran. Between these two masters of Xing Yi they ran a very successful body guarding business for many years – which in those days was a rough business, and real combat using a variety of weapons would occur frequently.

Li Neng Ran (1809-1890) and Guo Yun Shen (1839-1911) were two of the most influential masters in the modern Xing Yi story and the Xing Yi schools which descended from these great masters are what is today termed Hebei style. Although many practitioners of the art prefer to use the term 'Old Hebei Style' to distance themselves from modern Wu Shu where so-called Xing Yi 'forms' are unfortunately called Hebei Style by the Wu Shu practitioners. Very little, or no real Xing Yi flavour, character or principles can be seen within any of these alleged forms.

The Twelve Animals

The Animal characters (Xings) in our school are generally taught in the following order:

- Bear Eagle (Xiong Ying Xing)
- Snake (She Xing)
- Tiger (Hu Xing)
- Dragon (Long Xing)
- Chicken (Ji Xing)
- Horse (Ma Xing)
- Swallow (Yan Xing)
- Crocodile (Tuo Xing)
- Goshawk (Yao Xing)
- Flycatcher (Tai Xing)
- Monkey (Hou Xing)
- Turtle (Gui Xing)

From the list above it can be seen that there are:
- Five birds
- Three reptiles
- Four mammals *(Dragon represents Human Xing)*

Although this is a good order to teach the Animal Xings in, you will find that you may learn them in a different order, and depending on the class structure will just pick up bits of each animal here and there as the months and years roll on.

Just take the opportunity to learn as it arises without forethought, as you never know when you may be without a teacher for a length of time. Even when learning some aspects of the more advanced Animal Xings early in your training, you may not appreciate or comprehend what you are being taught at the time, but later on you will find that you will have those 'light-bulb' moments, and it will start to make sense to you. Just like small seeds being planted, can one-day blossom into huge trees.

The first six animals are sometimes called the more basic Xings (although there is nothing particularly basic about them) and the final six are the more advanced Xings. This is especially true with a few of the Animal strategies which are extremely difficult to embody properly, let alone master. Goshawk and Monkey are very advanced and many years of practice with a solid foundation in XingYi is required before being able to use these Xings properly, let alone being proficient with them in combat.

Each of the Animals in XingYi are indeed a unique fighting system in their own right, which provides the practitioner with a vast tool set of movements and strategies with which to defeat an opponent. Based upon how your opponent is moving and fighting, the XingYi adept, with a number of different Animal Xings under his belt, will be able to change his own strategy to better his chances of winning and gain the advantage.

This is quite a unique way of fighting in itself, and can somewhat baffle your opponent as you will be able to move and fight in a variety of ways. Being able to switch between the Animal Xings cleanly and seamlessly during combat is key to this overall strategy being effective.

To master all of the Animals in Xing Yi is a humongous task, and in the modern world is less likely to occur due to the time constraints of modern life.

You will need to put in many hours a day of practice time, with on-going contact with your teacher – so it is more likely in modern times that the Xing Yi adept will probably master only a few of the animals.

Although it is not unusual for modern teachers of Xing Yi to be able to teach all of the Animals to their students, they may not be proficient or comfortable using certain Xings when in a combat situation. Let's face it, you are going to fall back on your best strategies when in a fight, and will rely on what comes most naturally to you.

When the Xing Yi adept is able to comfortably fight with a number of different animal strategies then, depending upon the opponent, he will often start off in a fight with a strategy which is perhaps not the one that he is best at.

If the opponent happens to be a good fighter, then the Xing Yi adept will then switch his strategy to an animal he is better at. It is often the case that the Xing Yi fighter will keep his best fighting strategy closely concealed – as they wouldn't want any adversary to know what their best strategy is before a potential fight.

Remember, if you do find yourself in a fight, you need to be able to 'hang in the moment' during combat with no thoughts of the past or future for you to be most successful.

Just take what is 'given' to you in any potential combat situation, which is dependent upon yourself and your opponent(s), and the energy dynamics created at any given moment in time.

This is what we call 'Seeing the Heng' in Xing Yi, which comes out of your training and many hours of practice with various partners. Try to embody the famous Xing Yi saying which goes:

'See an opening, wait... See the Heng, strike!'

This is not something that can be directly taught, but will emerge out of your training and experience. If practicing with correct Xing Yi methods and strategy, this skill will certainly come through, and 'Seeing the Heng' will be 'in your bones' and become totally instinctive to you.

A myriad of variations and potential outcomes emerge continuously during any moment within a real combat situation. This is due to the continuous change of the energy (Chi) and intent (Yi) of the participants, and of the changes of the Xin - the energy surrounding them and which ultimately joins them.

Therefore, trying to think about what may come next, or what technique you are going to use just does not work, and is potential 'suicide' in a fight. So, just use and take what is given to you in the moment.

There is famous saying in Xing Yi which is used to describe the myriad of combat variations which can potentially come out of any given moment, which is:

'1 root, 1,000 branches, 10,000 endings'

This one phrase sums things up perfectly, with the 1 root being the moment that you find yourself and your opponent in, the 1,000 branches is referring to any of the potential methods which could be used when presented with the 1 root, and the 10,000 endings is referring to the myriad of potential endings of the encounter (10,000 here meaning somewhat infinite).

If you think about it, every time there is a movement between yourself and your opponent, it gives rise to another 1 root, and therefore another 1,000 branches — so the possibilities are endless and trying to think or plan your attack in advance is pointless and imaginary.

Not only will this slow you down — as you will be trying to think instead of naturally reacting, but the reality is that thinking and imagining just aren't practical, and don't work effectively in a fight (or in many other situations in life).

Thinking too much and analysing is the poor payback which we have evolved to our detriment as modern, civilised humans. So, a key tip is to practice cutting off your thoughts— both during all of your Xing Yi practice, and during other ancillary practices. In fact, it is good practice to attempt this during your everyday life when going about any task, however complicated or mundane.

You will be surprised by how much more efficiently your life will run, by just letting go of thinking, and by acting spontaneously and in the moment. Just follow your spirit, physicality and instincts, and you will not only have an easier life, but a more fun and enjoyable one as well.

My Xing Yi teacher, Damon Smith, wrote the first book in this series some 16 years ago with his book Xing Yi Bear Eagle. However, my last book Xing Yi Quan: A Study of Tai and Tuo Xing, in which I took a look into the fighting strategies of Tai Xing (Flycatcher) and Tuo Xing (Crocodile) somewhat jumped the order. So, I decided that if I was going to write any more books on Xing Yi, I would start back at the beginning and progress in some sort of order. Therefore this book is now going to take you on a journey into the fascinating strategy of Snake (She Xing).

Xing Yi Snake (She Xing)

'As the person advances, the steps advance –
one step, one strike.
When one branch moves,
hundreds of branches all follow...'

Snake, (She Xing) is a fascinating strategy to embody and use in your Xing Yi practice, and one which will give you a tool-set of fighting methods which range from medium to extremely close range, where you will find yourself body-to-body with your opponent.

The close range aspect of Snake is one of Xing Yi's best strategies if you find yourself on the ground and in a grappling situation. Xing Yi practitioner's prefer to be up on their feet and striking hard, but if things don't necessarily go to plan and you end up on the ground, or indeed on your feet but in a wrestling scenario, then you will find that She Xing tactics are very useful, and time invested in 'Yin She Xing' or 'Yin Snake' will give you some excellent skills with which to defend yourself.

There are two different types of snake which are embodied and used to great advantage within Xing Yi, and these are:

- *The Viper or 'Kuishe'* - Yang Snake
- *The Constrictor or 'Damang'* - Yin Snake

From the characters of these two snakes it should be obvious which one is used for medium-range fighting and which would best suit close-range encounters.

The viper uses quick, darting actions to strike into the range of its prey before bighting and injecting its venom – to do this the viper requires not only speed, but pin-point accuracy with its striking. This aspect of Snake Xing is very Yang in its nature and will actively seek to attack the opponent. Bright Jin (Ming Jin) is often used for these sharp, quick attacks, which flick out like a whip being uncoiled. To do this, energy is 'borrowed' in a number of different ways, with the peak power of the strike occurring upon impact, just like the final uncoiling of a whip, when the energy contained within it makes a cracking sound.

The constrictor is also a very quick snake when it comes to attacking, but is also a master of stealth and tracking. When in range of its prey it will want to get as close to it as possible, so it can coil its body around it to start squeezing and crushing. To do this the constrictor will often bite and hold on to its victim while the rest of the snake's long body carefully slips around and starts its crushing movements, this aspect of Snake Xing is very Yin in nature. The heavy, crushing movements of Yin Snake contain a lot of An Jin (Dark Jin), giving an extremely dense feel to its methods, in which the Xing Yi fighter is looking to smother and pin down the opponent's movements before various chokes are applied.

The characters of the two different types of snake presented here are indeed very different, and although many of the movements look very similar to the naked eye, there is without doubt a different feeling to the way in which the energy moves within the Xing Yi adepts body. The unique way in which these two snakes move, enables the Xing Yi fighter to apply their differing aspects, strategies and methods – and when their Xings come through in combat they really do become quite a formidable force.

Out of interest, one of the Xing Yi masters who taught my teacher was extremely good at Snake. Although he was good at all of the animals, he had a particular talent for this Xing. My teacher would tell me numerous stories about this master, and some of the incredible skills which came through him when he was fighting with and applying his snake strategy.

I have seen a picture of this master, who was quite small, but the power that he could generate was incredible, especially when using his Snake Xing. For some amusement, he once entered a martial arts tournament in China and decided to only use one technique from Yin Snake. He was so formidable at that one technique that he easily won the tournament, even though he was holding back the technique's power.

As already mentioned earlier in this book, the Yin aspect of Xing Yi has a very nurturing feel to it and will not actively seek to press an attack. This master was so good at Yin Snake that, as much bigger opponents would be trying everything to attack him with, he would be doing the opposite and possibly moving backwards while absolutely 'trashing' them – the fights would not last long.

My teacher always told me stories of this Old Hebei Style, Xing Yi group who were based near Beijing. They practice a traditional family branch of the art which is descended directly from Grand Master Guo Yun Shen. In fact the master who I have just discussed was not the highest ranking or most skilled within the group, as there was another master who was his teacher.

Nobody really knew about them as they were not interested in seeking fame, and were a private group of people. My teacher already had a martial arts CV as long as his arm when he met them, and had been practicing Xing Yi for many years with some very good masters. In fact he was already extremely experienced with Xing Yi, which was now his main fighting art (his experience in the art was the reason why they invited him to train with them). However, when he came upon this group and was invited to practice with them, he was amazed by their incredible skill and power – this was indeed a master-class in Xing Yi, with only a handful of students present (which is the traditional way), allowing my teacher to further refine his own Xing Yi skills and knowledge.

Within the Xing Yi syllabus, we often think and talk about Snake as being a fundamental Xing. This is in part because it is a fairly easy Xing to learn, which will enable the practitioner to gain an animal character to fight with early on in their training. It is also a very useful Xing to have, which will set you up with some really practical, fight stopping techniques. Therefore Snake can be taught to the student first or straight after Bear-Eagle *(Xiong Ying)*.

Having said this, although it is a character which you can gain some use out of fairly quickly, to get to the highest level of the character will be a challenge over many years, due to its incredible subtlety. Snakes have amazing sensing skills and are masters of minute movement, this can be observed within the change of their own energy and intent, and also in the way in which they pick up on the changes of the energy and intent of their prey, or even when they are being attacked.

During the many hours and years of practicing She Xing, you will need to take on and emulate these incredible skills – which you will need to nurture and refine for your use as an effective fighting strategy.

Snake Shaped Fists

As with pretty much all of the animal Xings which you will study within Xing Yi, Snake Xing has its own unique ways of striking and delivering power into the opponent.

Due to this fact and because She Xing can often be employed to deliver heavy strikes from unusual directions and positions, the fist *(Quan)* and palm *(Zhang)* are shaped to maximize the protection to your own hands, and to ensure that the striking power when emitting Jin occurs cleanly.

Protecting your own hands when attacking in Xing Yi is vital, both at the early stages in your training, when your body's alignments may not be perfect, and when you are more advanced and can deliver greater power. Although at the later stages in your training your hands should be well conditioned and stronger, with good structural alignment.

Most of the strikes in Xing Yi will not only be delivering heavy blows, with various Jins being employed to hurt your opponent, but more often than not will also have all of your body weight moving through your hand and into the target. Make sure that you take the early stages of your training slowly and carefully when learning to strike in this manner, as it is easy to cause damage to your own wrists and hands, which defeats the object of being able to strike hard, and can delay your progression within the art.

She Xing often uses the open palm instead of a closed fist, when striking in an upwards or downwards direction. Unlike the open palm that is used for classic Pi Quan striking (the position of the forward palm when holding San Ti), Snake strikes often use the sides of the hand. This is created by turning your hand 90 degrees from the classic Pi Quan open palm position, so that the side of your hand next to your little finger is facing downwards, and your thumb is now facing towards the sky.

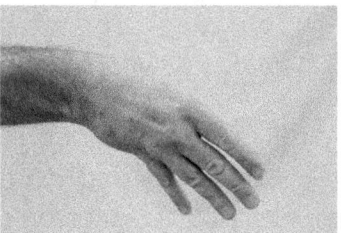 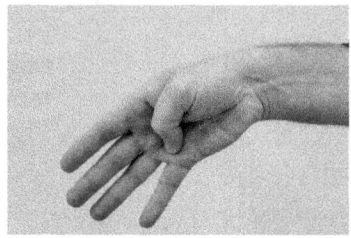

The thumb must now be tightly tucked into your palm, while the rest of your fingers point away from you. When striking upwards you must point your hand/fingers down with the wrist bent, which opens up the hard/compact, bony area on top of your hand (adjacent to your thumb). This will give you a much smaller surface with which to deliver your strikes with, so not only is it a strong structure that will protect your wrist and hand, but it will also ensure that maximum pain is delivered to your opponent. Much in the same way that Luo Xing Quan (conch shell shaped fist) delivers far greater pain, due to the small surface area of the extended finger when striking (see below). Note: other ways of forming the fist will be explored later.

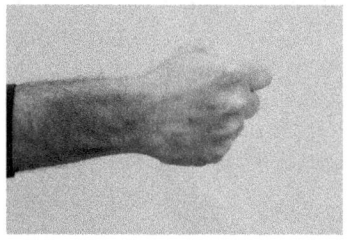 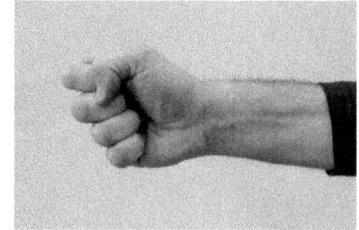

This unique formation of the hand/palm in She Xing is also used for control purposes, both to bind up the opponent before striking them (using Nui Da), and also when entering a grappling encounter. The hook which is formed between the base of the hand and the wrist produces a surface which is used to apply this aspect of Snake Xing, and is ideal for tying up the opponent, or to just stop them moving away easily.

Nui Da

Nui Da translates as *'bind-strike'*, and can be thought of as Xing Yi's very own way of approaching locking (Chin Na). The Xing Yi fighter may or may not be good at applying locks, but in the Xing Yi world view this is not a problem as you just want to keep striking the opponent. So, with Nui Da, if the lock works and it damages or hurts the opponent then great, but if it doesn't work then that's not a problem as you are looking for another opportunity to strike them.

More often than not you are not even looking for the lock to work, but to momentarily distract the opponent, or get a reaction out of them as they try to escape – so it is a way of setting up potential opportunities to land your next strike.

There is a lot of Nui Da employed when fighting with She Xing, where many of the movements will bind, hinder or stick onto the opponent while you follow up with heavy strikes, often into their groin, eyes or throat.

Mutually supportive Xing combinations

You will find that many of the animals in Xing Yi can be paired up with another animal, to give you a broader and more robust fighting strategy than if the animal were being used in isolation.

The most obvious example of this is the use of Bear-Eagle as a combined strategy, with the Bear methods being employed to fight at close range, and the Eagle methods being used for long range attacking and defence. Note: some schools of Xing Yi study these animals in isolation (Bear and Eagle), however in our school we study the Bear-Eagle as a joint strategy. There is a small Eagle which is native to Asia called the Bear-Eagle (Spizaetus Nipalensis in Latin), and this is the animal Xing which we are looking to emulate and study in our school. It is a small bird which will take on much larger prey than itself, so when it's at close range with large prey it will move much in the same way as a Bear, rolling with the motion of the struggling prey whilst hindering it's movements and striking with its talons. However, it doesn't matter if you view these animal strategies as separate animals or as the Bear-Eagle, as the fighting methods and strategies are the same in all schools of Xing Yi.

Another good example of mutually supportive Xing combinations would be to use Tai (Flycatcher) and Tuo (Crocodile) together as a wider and more complete strategy. These animal Xings were reputedly added to the Xing Yi syllabus by Master Li Neng Ran who was one of the founders of what we today call the Hebei school of Xing Yi (the other recognised founder being Master Guo Yun Shen).

For more information on this subject please refer to the following book- Xing Yi Quan: A Study of Tai and Tuo Xing.

The two types of snake which are presented to you in this book are no different in this respect, and they work extremely well together as a joint strategy. Yang Snake being used to fight at mid-range while striking hard into your opponent, and Yin Snake being utilised when the distance has been closed. Together they make up an excellent fighting strategy, whose methods cover many differing fighting angles and ranges during combat.

It is also worthy to note here that although Yin and Yang Snake indeed work very well as a joint strategy, Yang Snake and Bear Xing (Xiong) also work well together, with Bear Xing being utilised if the distance is shortened with an opponent.

Snake Energy Dynamics

She Xing strategy, as with all other strategies within Xing Yi, will make use of pretty much all of the ways of creating Jin (warrior strength). However, through your practice of the art you will observe that each animal strategy will make more use of certain ways of creating Jin, and some of the other Jins will take more of a back seat. Note: see the Appendix for a full list and explanation of the eight prevalent Jins which are used within Xing Yi.

To create the twisting and coiling structures which are so characteristic with She Xing, you will need to be able to manipulate your energy to generate lots of expanding and contracting spirals. Tsuan Jin is Xing Yi's prime way of creating spirals with the energy potential of the body, so it will be no surprise that She Xing methods and structures are formed by making full use of this way of generating power. This can be seen throughout most of the Snake methods, when fighting or just moving your structure with this fundamental Xing.

These spirals can be felt to move from big to small and vice versa, depending on the application of specific strategic movements. It is also worth noting that these spirals can also move in a bi-directional way, just as in the standard use of Tsuan Quan from the Five Elements Xing Yi. This way of manipulating energy has a very unique feel to it, and you often hear people describing it as being like the energy created when an awl is in use.

Beng Jin is used as a prime way to create the crushing power when fighting with Yin Snake. In the same manner as the constrictor seeks to crush its prey, you will also be able to effectively squeeze and crush your opponent while employing the 'compression phase' of this way of creating Jin. This is also combined with Tsuan Jin to coil and twist around your opponents structure, while simultaneously squeezing and crushing them.

It is worth mentioning here, that if you add Tsuan Jin to your standard Beng Jin strikes, then it has the added advantage of making your strikes stick to the opponent. This is useful when striking powerfully with Beng Quan, to ensure that your strike is not wasted and does not slip off of the target.

Pi Jin striking is not seen in all of She Xing's techniques, but one of this animal's most famous strikes uses Pi Jin by the bucket load. This is the strike which starts low, but hits upwards and very powerfully with the side of the forearm, wrist or hand as they are ascending at speed. Although at the end of this heavy upward strike, you can use Fan Jin to reverse the flow of your energy and strike again using Pi Jin in a downwards direction –

this tends to happen if you find that your strike has gone high, so you take advantage of this and instantly strike again with a downwards Pi, using the bottom edge of your forearm, wrist of hand. You will find that this normally lands on the opponent's neck or collar bone area.

She Xing controlling methods will use Kou Jin and Nian Jin to turn the opponent's structure or slow down their movements, putting them at a disadvantage and allowing you to gain a better position on them before striking. Although, when using Yin Snake strategy and you are body-to-body with your opponent, Beng Jin can also be effectively used to control and hinder them. This is especially true when you are compressing part of their body between your arms and your own body, which is extremely effective.

Of course, Heng Jin is used in She Xing as it is in all areas of Xing Yi. This is a somewhat specialist Jin as it is fundamental to ensuring your Xin(g) Yi works. This relates to the energetic results of combined Xin and 'seeing the Heng' which is very difficult to try and describe in words, so you will need to learn and experience what this means through the many hours of two man practice that will be required in your training. Combined Xin is referring to the joining of your own Xin and your opponents, which only happens upon contact.

Over time you will come to find that the Jins which are employed in Xing Yi are rarely used in isolation, but will combine or support each other in numerous ways.

Shi Er Xing Jiao Shou (Twelve Animals Fighting)

To learn how to fight with She Xing or with any of the animals in Xing Yi, you will need to invest time in your two man practice. Jiao Shou is the term used for fighting in Xing Yi and is the platform upon which you can really start to breathe life into your practice. This is where you hone your skills, and many hours of practice will be required with each of the animals to become proficient at them.

As the old saying goes – 'you can't make and omelette without breaking some eggs', and many mistakes will be made along the way with this important and essential part of your training. Do not be put off by this, as the more mistakes that you make, the more learning and experience you are taking on, and it is often the case that the person who loses more during the early stages of their Jiao Shao training, will end up be a more proficient and well-rounded fighter in the long run. Just play and experiment with what is given to you in any of these encounters, as each person that you train with will move differently, and ultimately will give you varying skills with which to deal with a variety of situations.

In our school of Xing Yi we start to learn how to slot some of the more basic animal movements into our Five Elements Jiao Shao in the earlier stages of our training. This serves as a taster for how they work before we move onto the more advanced methods in the animals practice. Doing this will clearly show you how the animal methods are more subtle and effective than the Five Elements Xing Yi.

Go careful with your training partners, as you want to really help each other to learn and understand Xing Yi on deeper and more subtle levels, and of course you really don't want to start damaging your friends. If you just go out to kill each other every time you practice, then you may find that you miss out on much of the subtle levels that may be experienced, and this type of training will not allow you to experiment as much.

You can see this in nature when young Tiger cubs fight with each other to effectively learn how to defend themselves, before real fights occur during their adulthood. They are not trying to hurt each other, but will spend hours, rolling, pushing, hindering and nipping each other. This allows the necessary time for the cubs to let the experience gained through this engagement with their siblings seep into their bones – to the point that they will move effortlessly when the time comes for real action, which can quite easily mean life or death for them.

An experienced teacher (Sifu) is required when starting out on this stage of your training, and this is to ensure that you are adhering to the methods and strategies of the animal which you are using to fight with. When flustered it is easy to fall back on your instincts, and the animal strategy that you are best at. However, this would defeat the object of the exercise, as you will be practicing to learn how to fight with differing strategies, dependent upon the animal Xing which you are attempting to get better at. So pay close attention to how you are moving and reacting, to ensure that you keep each animal strategy 'pure'. It is a big mistake to mix up the animal strategies when fighting, as doing this will cause the now tarnished strategy to fail – so remember that they must be kept separate.

If you watch a practitioner who is experienced in Xing Yi fighting, you will see them switch between animal Xings effortlessly, and they will be doing this at the appropriate moment during combat. But if you observe them carefully, you will notice that they don't mix up the differing animal strategies. At this stage of their Xing Yi, they would have learnt to change their strategy, the way that they are moving, and their fighting intent without forethought. This is the advanced level of Xing Yi that you are aspiring to attain, the results of which are devastatingly effective when applied in combat.

So to round off, and in the context of this book, to learn to fight with either Yin or Yang Snake, and then to combine these strategies to greater effect, you must stick to the individual principles of each Xing. Then you will eventually reap the benefits of your labour, to be proficient in the unique and very effective fighting strategy of She Xing.

Yang Snake (Yang She Xing)

'The emitting is to severe the centre...'

The Xing Yi masters of old embodied and added two different Snake Xings (characters) to this living art, which have their own unique strategies for dealing with opponents or prey species. These are often quite simply termed, Yin and Yang Snake (or Yin She Xing and Yang She Xing).

Yang She Xing is a very useful strategy to use when you are fighting at a mid-range position with an opponent. From the fighting range which is used by Yang Snake, you will find that you are able to stay at a reasonably safe distance from any attacks, but are also able to close in on your opponent quickly to strike.

The Xing Yi fighter using Yang Snake strategy seeks to embody the tried and tested movements of the viper, and as such, your attacks become crisp and fast, striking into any opponent at lightning speed. Strikes are aimed at some of the softer areas of the body and, if the strike lands cleanly, are often fight-stoppers.

Prime targets which present themselves are the opponent's eyes, throat and most parts of the neck. Moving lower the soft area under the armpits become a good target, as do the flanks of their body, which will include strikes to the ribs, liver, and kidneys if the opponent is turned away from you. At the lower extremities of the opponents body, the fierce upward strikes which are so characteristic of She Xing seek to target the groin and inside of the legs – of course this strong upwards strike works equally as well when delivered under the opponent's chin.

The viper is an extremely aggressive animal, and this is the mindset which you are seeking to embody when using this strategy. Coupled with this aggression and quick striking ability, is the requirement to hit the target with a good degree of accuracy. If you are using your fingers to strike into the opponent's eyes, then you really don't want to be striking hard with your fingertips into any of the heavy or bony areas around the head, as it is possible to break your own fingers. This is especially true when striking with your body weight moving behind your hand. (See photos below for finger positions).

Note: when it comes to striking in Xing Yi, the overriding strategy isn't normally that concerned with accuracy, but instead you just seek to strike the opponent hard, irrespective of whether it hits an exact target on their body.

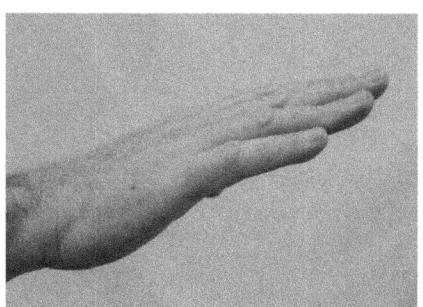 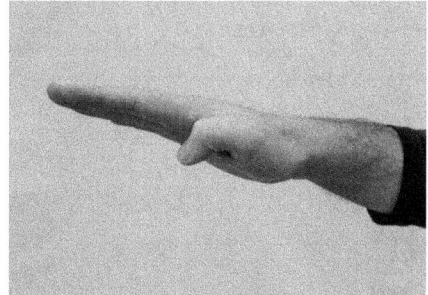

But unless you have amazing conditioning in your fingers, you could be asking for trouble when using the finger jabs which are characteristic of many of the Snake strikes, and the last thing that you want to be doing in a fight, is damaging the prime striking weapon of your body.

For this reason, a lot of the striking in Yang Snake makes use of the Bright Jin (Ming Jin) style of power generation. Bright Jin is not as heavy as Dark Jin striking, but instead uses quick bursts of power, where the energy speeds up whilst uncoiling, just as a whip uncoils, to deliver maximum power at the end of its motion – when you hear the whip's 'crack' sound. This also adds to the speed and 'flavour' of your striking, which needs to move in a fast and darting motion, embodying the movements of the viper.

This same motion must be applied to your own energy to be able to deliver strikes in this manner effectively. Using Bright Jin in this way, allows you to hold your body weight back whilst delivering strong blows into your opponent, and if the target is their eyes, then it can easily be understood how effective this type of striking can be. However, it would really have to be a life and death situation to use this kind of strategy on someone, as the consequences are, of course, not great for the person being struck. So, when practicing any strikes to the eyes with your training partners, go very slow and only practice them if you have a decent level of control over your strikes. It may also be worth buying some strong safety glasses to protect your eyes.

Another way of forming the fist when striking with She Xing is to retract the end of your fingers, so that you are striking with the joints that are next to your knuckles. (See below).

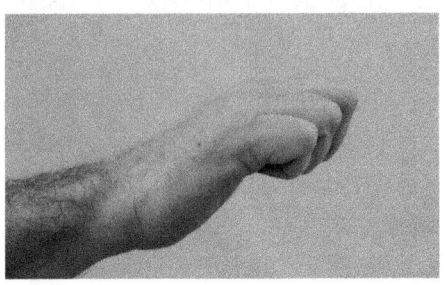 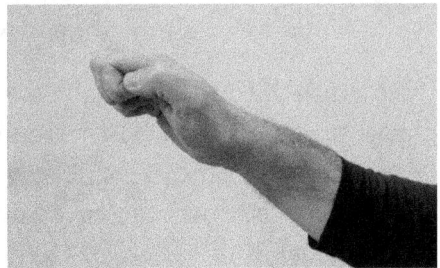

Within Xing Yi, this unique way of holding the fist is only seen in She Xing and will give your hand much more stability and strength for striking, than if you were to have your fingers fully extended. It is worth noting here that even when your fingers are fully extended, there is still a very slight curve to their structure – as in all of Xing Yi's structures throughout the body, nothing is ever truly straight, but has a roundness to it (however subtle this may be). To the untrained eye this is not always obvious, but to someone who has been trained in Xing Yi and has a good understanding of Xing Yi's physical and energetic structures, it is quite clear.

This strength throughout the Xing Yi adepts structure comes from the famous San Ti Shi (Three Body Posture), which when applied correctly, turns every part of the body into a mutually supportive structure which generally acts in threes. Over the years and long hours of practicing Xing Yi, you will come to appreciate how a well formed Three Body Posture gives you a very robust structure, not only in your physical body, but also in your energy (Chi) and spirit (Xin). Also, all elements that go into forming a good structure support each other, so that any movement in any part of your body will be supported by all the other parts – this gives rise to Xing Yi's whole body movement where you will literally be moving as one solid unit. The opposite of this, and a key way to see if someone is practicing Xing Yi well or not, is if the practitioner is just using isolated parts of their anatomy to move and strike.

Although Xing Yi is an art which never holds onto, or grips an opponent with the hand, this rule is often broken with some of She Xing's methods, where you can use your hand at lighting speed to 'bite' into the opponent in exactly the same way that a constrictor will bite and hold onto its prey at high speed.

Yang Snake (Yang She Xing)

When using this strategy your hand will close around the opponent and your fingers will need to dig into their skin. Think of controlling the opponent's arm by wrapping your hand around their wrist, with your palm on one side of their arm and your fingers on the other side, and pushed hard into their skin. This stops them from getting away, and will allow you time to either follow up with strikes with the other hand (or possibly the same hand), or move in closer to grappling range. However, if you move into close range it would be time to switch strategy and slip into Yin Snake mode, we will explore this further in a later chapter of this book.

This way of using the hand to literally 'bite' the opponent is, of course, not limited to just their arms, but can be applied to most areas of the opponent's body. The flank of the body or neck are good locations to seize onto your opponent. If your grip is strong enough and you have managed to get a good hold of their skin (and/or tendons), then you can also wrench hard to tear skin or cause internal damage.

The twisting and coiling motion of the Snake can clearly be seen in the movements of the Xing Yi fighter, when applying this strategy correctly. This opens up interesting and unusual angles of attack with which to immobilise and strike your opponent. One of the most unique techniques which comes out of using Snake strategy is the long upward moving strike, which hits with the side of the hand and/or wrist.

The coiling and lowering of the body's structure/chi whilst moving in this manner, puts you in a position where the energy potential of your body will want to move in an upwards direction (the energy, literally urges the technique out into your structure). Not only that, but the initial coiling and dropping of the body will almost always put you in a place where there is a direct

striking line into the target. Note: the twisting and coiling of the body is achieved by mostly using Beng Jin and Tsuan Jin, to create the expansion/compression and spirals within your energy, and hence your physical body follows. The upward strike uses a lot of Pi Jin, which is directed up to strike into the opponent like a rising axe blade.

This allows you to move from down to up rapidly, and the strike which comes up and out, into your opponent, can have a tremendous amount of power in it. As mentioned previously, this strike is normally targeting the groin area of your opponent, and as in all Xing Yi methods you will look to strike through their position. If you can deliver a large amount of power, then this technique would not only strike their groin, but will also move up into their pelvic region, causing severe trauma and damage.

The famous Xing Yi saying of 'move to the right to enter the left, move to the left to enter the right' is clearly seen and used throughout She Xing methods, and it is often this strategy which opens up the strong lines of attack with which to take advantage of any adversary.

This is a fundamental strategy in Xing Yi and is therefore not isolated to She Xing, but can be seen throughout all of Xing Yi's different animals, and also in the Five Elements Xing Yi (Wu Xing).

The viper's crisp and accurate movements can often be seen moving to the left then striking right, etc. We must make use of this strategy, coupled with strong lines of intent to drive hard, and at times ferocious attacks. Remember to never let up once the attack is on, do not give your opponent a second chance to get back into the fight, and keep striking them at every opportunity, with as much force as possible. This is Xing Yi's way.

Some of the words that fit the character of this ferocious strategy are: winding and coiling, strong and flexible, parting and entering, whipping and recoiling, and of course tracking and stealth.

Remember that Xing Yi is an extremely subtle art, and the tracking and stealth side of this animal's character can easily be overlooked, so make sure that you 'feel and sense' what the opponent is going to do, or how they are moving. This comes from many years of practice and cannot really be taught to you in isolation. It comes from your two-man practice, and from having a good teacher who can show you how to move and act correctly, and not from words alone – which will always fall short of truly transmitting such a subtle teaching.

國立故宮博物院藏品

Yin Snake (Yin She Xing)

'When upper and lower move, the centre will attack,
When the centre moves, the upper and lower support...'

Yin Snake can be thought of as Xing Yi's best strategy for very close-range fighting, and is used to a large extent if the Xing Yi fighter finds himself in a grappling encounter. In fact, for this fascinating strategy to work effectively, you will need to move into extremely close range, where you find yourself body-to-body with your opponent. Being based on the hunting and fighting strategy of the constrictor, you can really see where the close quarter methods derive from, especially if you sit for a while and watch these animals while they hunt and dispatch their prey.

The internet has a lot of good videos of constrictors in action, so it is well worth spending some time studying their movements (Yan Xing) as you will be looking to emulate these in yourself, enabling you to use this strategy effectively.

Note: Yan Xing (study of Xing) is a term used by practitioners when they go out into nature to study the characters of wild animals, especially if the animals are the ones which we are studying under the Xing Yi umbrella.

Of course, not everyone will be lucky enough to be able to study the animals in Xing Yi for real, so instead you can watch the thousands of videos that are available on the Internet when studying a specific animal's Xing (character) – you will be surprised at what you can learn by watching and emulating in yourself what these animals have to offer. Put your thoughts and ego to one side and just take what is being given to you by the animals, then bring this back into yourself and the way in which your body/energy moves during your practice. This truly adds another layer of understanding to your practice, and it is exactly what the masters of old would have done themselves.

All constrictors hunt and protect themselves much in the same manner, and this can be broken down into the three basic areas of:

- *Using stealth and minute movements to track their prey.*
- *Biting and/or using torsion against the side of the prey's body to limit their movements.*
- *Constricting and crushing the prey until they pass out.*

So let's take a look at these three areas in some more detail and try and lay some foundation for this unique strategy. Remember that the Yin aspect of an animal's strategy as viewed in Xing Yi, has a much more nurturing feel to it. This means that instead of striking out to the opponent, or trying to get a reaction out of them by actively seeking opportunities, which is a more Yang strategy, you will be generally moving in and around their movements and slipping through the gaps when they present themselves (these can be gaps in their physical structure, their energy or their intent). This is the nurturing Yin aspect, and it has to be understood that this is totally different to the much more Yang quality, which is utilised when fighting with Yang Snake.

You will also come to understand that the three areas mentioned above are all interlinked with each other. These skills therefore overlap, and in post-analysis of your Xing Yi you will be able to see how they rarely act in isolation. For example, you may be constricting whilst sensing/feeling for any changes of movement or intent of the opponent.

Snakes are the masters of stealth, and this attribute can be seen in all types of snake without exception. Yin She Xing strategy makes extensive use of stealth and sensing, and it is this aspect of Yin Snake that really breathes life into this strategy, during your practice, and in any combat situation.

This is quite an unusual skill to acquire, but once learnt you will without doubt be way more effective when applying Yin Snake in a fight. You must make use of your senses and energy, to literally feel within the other person and pick-up on any movements which are going on inside them, no matter how minute these may be. As you will be generally body-to-body with your opponent, you will be able to get information fed into you from all over.

You must have great patience when doing this, just close off your mind and try not to get flustered or panic. A key point now arises, and one which is crucial to ensuring that Yin Snake strategy works. You must only move when the opponent moves, and this may only be the tiniest of changes within the opponent's energy or intent. Also when they stop moving, you stop – unless there is an obvious chance of striking.

This is quite a hard skill to master, but once you get a feel for it you will be surprised at the effect that this will have, and when you are also moving in the correct manner, you will find that you start to get the upper hand on the opponent effortlessly.

This is exactly what constrictors do when keeping body-to-body with their prey, and they act as if they have all the time in the world, often waiting for their prey to move before slipping around them.

This presents another key point, which is that by using correct methods and moving only as and when the opponent dictates, then the opponent unknowingly ends up deciding on their own downfall. You don't really have to put any thought into it at all – just keep tracking and moving appropriately into the gaps in their defence as they move.

Before long they will get themselves in a bad structural position, where you will be able to take full advantage and continue squeezing and crushing, while using the Dark Jin way of creating force and applying it into them.

Also, when the opponent breathes out, follow their movements (their rib cage compressing) and keep the crushing pressure on, which will mean that they will slowly be taking shorter and shorter breaths, as they won't be able to expand their chest again, and this will ultimately deplete their oxygen intake.

This is one of Xing Yi's methods of allowing the opponent to choose how they are going to be beaten, which saves you having to think about it – it is as if they have defeated themselves.

However, this concept is not just utilised by Yin Snake strategy, throughout all of Xing Yi's techniques there are many subtle ways in which you allow the opponent to decide how they are going to be beaten, allowing you to react to any given combat situation which presents itself. You just take what the opponent 'gives you' in the moment and without forethought.

You want to be using this same Snake method to apply pressure to any part of the opponent's body which you are coiled around. This could be with your torso, your legs wrapping around the opponent's legs/body, or your arms which will be moving in exactly the same manner as a snakes body, when wrapping around a branch or its prey. When moving in the correct manner, while also employing She Xing techniques and strategy, you will find that your arms naturally coil around the opponent and will more often than not end up coiled around and constricting their throat.

A lot of Tsuan Jin and Beng Jin is used throughout your body to create these coiling and crushing movements. The application of Tsuan and Beng Jin together, enables you to create many spirals throughout your body and chi, with the compression phase of Beng Jin squeezing the spirals tighter together and making them more compact – your intent will also be directing these dense/compressed spirals into your opponent. Of course, to slightly release and slip around your opponent, you will be using the expansive phase of Beng Jin whilst combined with Tsuan Jin – enabling the spirals to grow in size, before compressing and constricting once again.

Nian Jin is also used to a large extent to help pin down the opponent's movements as they become hindered every time they move by the torsion between your body/limbs and their own. Tiny circles and spirals are created to achieve this, which act between the surface of your skin and theirs. This slows down and hinders their movements, while also sapping the power out of them, allowing you to keep taking the advantage.

As with Yang Snake (viper) the constrictor will also initially bite at speed, but they will then hold onto their prey. So there is no problem with seizing and digging your fingers into your opponent to further hinder him from moving or escaping. As with Xing Yi's Nui Da (bind-strike) strategy, this is just a means to an end, and you are not overly concerned if the opponent struggles and breaks free of your grip, as his actions will only serve to give you more opportunities to either get a better position on him to carry on grappling, or a clear line of attack may present itself to strike him cleanly.

Going to Ground

People who are trained in Xing Yi will almost certainly prefer to stay on their feet whilst in a combat situation. Xing Yi is a striking art, and as such its practitioner's love to stay upright while striking with heavy, fight-stopping blows into their opponents. However, if things don't go to plan and you do find yourself having to go to the ground with an opponent, then Yin Snake is the strategy that most suits fighting from the floor.

There are other animal strategies that work well from certain positions whilst on the ground, but none are as good as Yin Snake for hindering the opponent's movements and for fighting while you are horizontal. Therefore, time invested in getting to a decent level of ability with Yin Snake is well worth the effort – you never know when you will end up in a ground fight, and you will need to be able to at least protect yourself if the situation arises.

This is especially true in the modern world where so many people are practicing ground fighting arts like Brazilian Jiu-Jitsu, so it is highly likely that you may come up against someone who has been trained in this manner.

Fighting from the floor is completely different from when you are on your feet, the muscles used and the energy dynamics which arise will not be familiar, unless you have spent some time on the floor practicing with a training partner.

Most of the techniques which you have learnt while on your feet can be rendered useless, and it can be very difficult to generate power (Jin) unless practiced. Even striking with a simple punch using Beng Jin will be more difficult if you are not familiar with generating strikes whilst lying down, without your energy and body-weight in motion. However, many of the methods within XingYi can be adapted for ground fighting – although you will need a teacher to explain and show you how to do this, as it can be an incredibly subtle practice.

Once you have gained an aptitude for using She Xing ground fighting methods, which will enable you to deliver heavy strikes while on the floor, then you will definitely have an advantage in this area as opposed to someone who may be able to apply good hindering and locking techniques, but may not be used to being struck so hard.

To sum up, some words that really characterise this dangerous predator are: winding and coiling, containing and constricting, following and absorbing. All of which are embodied with control, great subtlety and stealth.

宋李迪筆

花香鳥語注韶熙總是東皇一氣
施不藉畫禪真法眼河陽妙蹟
孰誰知 乾隆戊寅御題

國立故宮博物院藏品

She Xing Applications

'Thus when attacked you will not provide openings, and when pressed hard you will not become disarrayed...'

In the following pages I have chosen to show a selection of bare hand applications for She Xing, which will hopefully enable you to get a feel for the flavour of how snake strategy can be applied in your Xing Yi practice. This is just a small sample of possible Snake methods, and all of the methods shown here can be applied in numerous ways.

I have purposely moved away from showing any applications with weapons, as the movements and strategy become extremely subtle. As such, the flavour of an animals Xing can be completely lost in static photographs, unless you have some experience of weapons training.

It is also very difficult to portray the barehand flavour and strategy of any martial art, let alone Xing Yi in static pictures.

Therefore, I have purposefully shown most attacks throughout this book from standard straight and hook punches. It is clearer to see the application in photographs when using this platform, as opposed to the attacker using advanced Xing Yi techniques which are not visible to the naked eye.

All applications shown in this book will use the protocol of – the person on the left of the first photo in an application being Person A, and the person on the right being Person B.

She Xing Application 1

A grabs hold of B and is preparing to strike with a right punch. B moves to his right while simultaneously grabbing hold of A's left hand. Note: there is a slight arc to this move from B, which comes from his body as much as his arms, this is employed to ensure that A's hand and wrist are twisted.

B has also moved his weight back sharply, which has a 'jolting' effect on A's structure - this is to disrupt A's attack and stop him from throwing his punch effectively. (As a minimum, this will take some power out of it).

B's body now turns to his left while he keeps control of A's right hand,

which is held against his shoulder. B's right arm is simultaneously slipping over the top of A's left arm, just as a constrictor coils around a branch. Note: you must ensure that there are no gaps between your arm and the opponents when doing this. You need to use all of your body to apply this move correctly, and not just your arm in isolation. For this method to work it is also important to keep the opponents arm straight, if they bend their arm at the elbow then it will not 'go-on' easily, if at all.

B now drops his weight and structure heavily, with his right arm pointing towards the floor. Note: B's left hand is staying high and is still controlling and twisting A's hand and wrist, this is in the same manner as the snake biting into its prey.

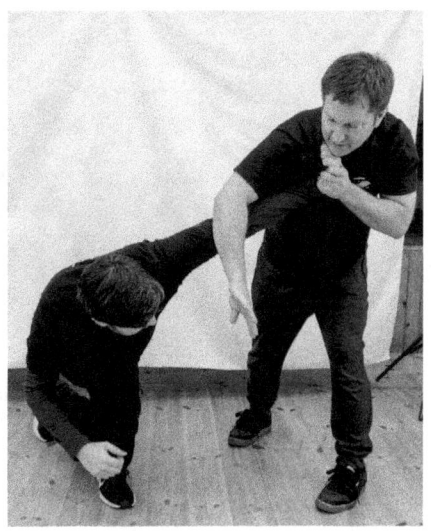

'A' drops to the floor to try and relieve the pressure which is being applied to the joints in his arm, this technique is very effective and puts a huge amount of pressure on the wrist, elbow and shoulder joints. It is incredibly painful when applied correctly, and if B was to sharply drop his weight down then it would be easy to break one of A's joints. Note: be very careful and go slowly when practicing this movement on your training partners.

B decides to follow up his attack and steps into A's position using the 'Jin' footwork (entering), he is simultaneously striking upwards under A's chin with the top side of his forearm – using Pi Jin.

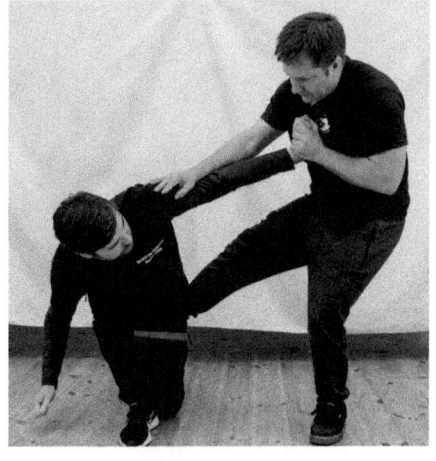

The last photo shows a different attack where B has decided to use a Pi Jin kick with his right foot into A.

Note: A's arm is still being controlled so that he can't move away from the kick.

Xing Yi - She Xing

She Xing Application 2

Person A grabs hold of B and prepares to punch with a high right. Person B evades by moving to his left slightly while using his left hand to cover A's attack. Note: B is using a very light touch on A's arm to allow the attack to pass by him, this is called 'Tseh' in Xing Yi which means to 'flank'.

As A's attack moves forward, B continues to position himself to strike. Once A is in range and has no real defence, B strikes hard using an upward Pi Jin strike into A's groin.

B is using Yang She Xing strategy, which enables him to strike while maintaining a slight distance from A.

She Xing Application 3

Person A grabs hold of B's wrists and is looking to go into a clinch. Instead of struggling with A, person B uses his dragon body to narrow his structure and drive himself forwards and into person A. B is also using a spiral which is coiling upwards, and this enables B to strike A with his right elbow under the chin.

Note: The strike to A's chin happens during B's movement and is not the end result. The strike and the application of the choke happens all in one motion.

B's right arm now slips around the back of A's head/neck. He then proceeds to step forward, into A's space while coiling around him. B's structure is twisting and dropping while simultaneously applying pressure to A's throat and neck.

Note: the dropping and twisting of B's structure adds a lot of weight and torsion onto A's neck.

It can also be seen that A's right arm is also seized and twisted by B to increase the torsion and further distort his position (see last page). The technique shown here is using Yin She Xing strategy, which seeks to coil and crush the opponent.

Remember that once A has been hindered, you will be presented with many potential options to progress the attack, so just hang in the moment and see what comes next. For example, if the headlock/choke is 'on' effectively, you may decide to carry on choking. If he starts struggling and finds a way out, just let him while following up with heavy strikes as he tries to regather himself.

You may also be able to drop him to the ground from this final position and follow him down to carry on attacking, or stay on your feet and kick him. Let the opponent decide what is coming next, and just take what is presented to you in any given moment.

She Xing Application 4

Person A attacks B with a left high punch. B must move quickly here and simultaneously slips (Tseh) A's attack down the side of his right arm which is coiling upwards.

Once in range B coils down and under A's arm, a striking angle has opened up to B as A's groin will be unprotected for an instant. Note: it is not obvious from the photos, but B has to cover his descent, so as not to be hit by A's right fist. To do this B's right hand lowered to go between his face and A's fist whilst coiling under A's arm. B could have used his left hand to cover, but if he had done this he wouldn't have been able to strike upwards on his follow up attack.

B now changes his attack and instantly uses an upwards Snake Pi Jin strike between A's legs. This attack which is so characteristic of She Xing is very effective and will cause a great deal of pain to person A if it lands correctly.

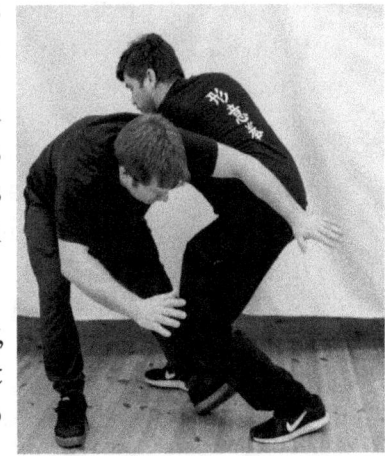

Even if this strike doesn't hit the target solidly, person A has no option but to try and move out of its way – this will often give person B time to strike again.

She Xing Application 5

Person B has seized and twisted A's wrist, and is seeking to apply a Yin Snake Nui da method to bind-up A's arm.

However, A has raised his elbow which will ensure that person B struggles to apply the lock to A's arm. Note: In Xing Yi we are not worried if the lock 'goes on' or not, and will be applying Nui da strategy instead. This means that if the lock doesn't work it's not a problem, and you will use the moment that they are struggling to escape, to attack them.

Person B knows that the arm lock is not going to work, so he twists A's hand and wrist in an anti-clockwise direction.

Note: if the opponent raises there elbow to escape the arm lock, then you should follow up immediately by twisting their wrist.

Their wrist will be vulnerable and you can apply the twist to get a reaction out of them as they struggle to move and relieve the pain. This is the exact moment to strike them, so do not delay and strike instantly.

While keeping hold of person A's twisted hand, person B now strikes using a Snake Tsuan variant which slips through a thin gap to A's chin/face.

As the line of attack is slipping under A's arm it will have an element of stealth about it, as it will be difficult for person A to see the strike coming until the last moment.

She Xing Application 6

Person A attacks person B with a left punch. Using Snake strategy B joins with A's attack by using the palm of his right hand, which slips along the underside of A's attack. Upon contact, B is using Nian Jin to slow down and take a lot of the energy out of A's attack.

Note: There is also a lot of strength in B's position which comes from having a well formed three body posture. B can use his structure like a wedge which acts against the floor and underside of A's arm, and which will disrupt A's position – in this case A is being moved to his right which is opening up his left flank for an attack by B. In fact the deeper A strikes, the more his position/structure will be disrupted.

As soon as the striking line opens up, person B switches to an attack and strikes A with a left punch employing a combination of Beng and Tsuan Jin – this is so characteristic of Snake Xing striking, which contains a lot of coiling and twisting energy.

She Xing Application 7

Person A attacks person B with a high left punch. Person B flanks the attack (Tseh) while simultaneously covering and taking control of A's arm and body, at the wrist and shoulder.

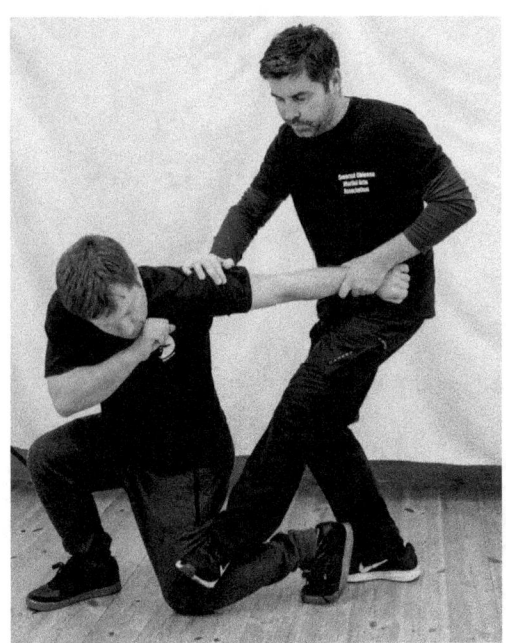

As B moves forward to slip past A's attack he is also raising his left foot and preparing to strike into A with a kick/stamp to his knee using Tsuan Jin.

Note: if delivered correctly and with good timing, this kick will cause a huge amount of damage to A's knee. Therefore go steady when practicing this kicking method on your training partners – a friend of mine had a similar technique applied to him in a real fight, and almost thirty years later he is still having problems with his knee.

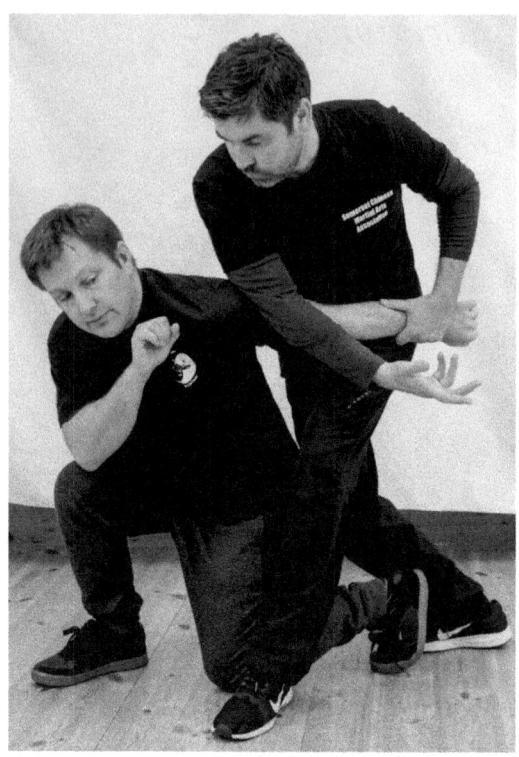

As soon as A drops down to the floor, B follows up with his next attack without hesitation.

In this instance B has decided to follow up with a She Xing strike with the edge of his forearm, up and through A's chin/head which incorporates Pi Jin.

Note: while delivering this strike B has still maintained control of A's arm and position, leaving him with little chance of defending himself.

He has seized tightly onto A's left arm, in the same manner as a snake would bite its prey.

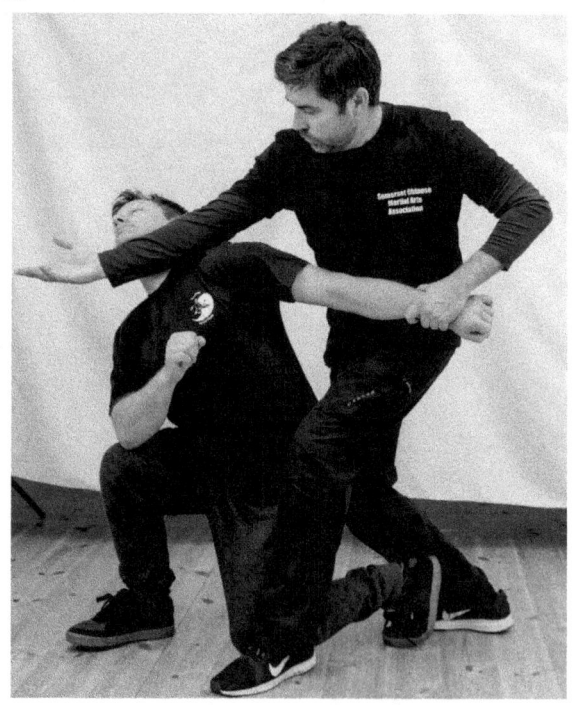

She Xing Application 7

She Xing Application 8

This short set of photos shows how a few She Xing methods can be linked together in application.

Person A is attacking B with a high left punch. B meets A's attack with the outside of his right arm. B then strikes towards A's eyes while simultaneously applying an appropriate amount of pressure to the inside of A's arm. This has the effect of diverting A's attack slightly so that it goes off of course. Note: do not apply too much pressure to the attackers arm. This is not a 'block' but is instead using the Xing Yi principle of simultaneous attack and defence.

The counter attack from person B causes A to flinch and move his head away from the strike.

Person A now retaliates with a right Beng Chuan, B senses this and withdraws slightly (Tui) while covering A's attack with his right arm/palm.

Once person A's attack is in a safe place, person B immediately attacks with a high She Xing strike, using his left fingers to attack A's eyes.

Note: it doesn't matter if this strike lands or not, as person A must react to get out of the way of the strike to his eyes – most of the time this will create an opportunity for you to strike again, and if appropriate you must follow up with your next attack without forethought to take the advantage.

Person B now moves forward and strikes person A with an uppercut to his chin, using Tsuan Jin. Note: while advancing into person A, person B has dropped his left arm to cover A's arm/position while simultaneously striking.

The last two moves from the Tsuan into the headlock, are carried out all in one motion.

After striking person A with Tsuan Jin, person B steps into A while simultaneously wrapping his right arm around A's neck. He then uses Tsuan and Beng Jin combined, while dropping his body-weight, to twist up and crush person A's neck.

Note: this is Beng Jin during its 'compression' phase, which will tightly squash person A's head between your arms and body. At the same time the Tsuan Jin will apply a twisting motion along person A's neck vertebrae.

She Xing Application 8

She Xing Application 9

This is a very useful Snake method to use if you are being attacked from behind, as it allows you to cover yourself while turning. However, it must be applied quickly for it to be effective.

Person A is about to attack B with a right punch. Person B has noticed this and immediately turns towards A by using a 'twisted root' and by coiling his body.

Person B's left arm has travelled in a fairly large arc, which first goes up and then drops down in front of him. Note: more often than not, this circular motion will at some point make contact with the attackers arm, enabling you to either control or knock it away from you.

As soon as person B contacts A's arm he immediately strikes out with his right hand, just as the Viper strikes its prey.

In this instance B's fingers are striking person A's eyes, but the follow up strike from B could have also been modified to attack anywhere on A's head or throat.

She Xing Application 10

Person B attacks A with a left Beng Chuan, while A is facing away from him. Person A has sensed/spotted this and turns while covering with his right hand/arm. Note: this is a similar turn as in Application 9, where the covering arm moves in an arc. However, in this version person A is stepping in a circular motion, which moves him away from B's line of attack.

Person A's right arm covers B's attack at the forearm. Note: there is little or no pressure applied to B's arm, this ensures that the minimum amount of information is given to person B, and therefore nothing for him to

react from. Person A has chosen to use this strategy so as to keep person B close to him, ensuring that he will set up B for his forthcoming elbow strike.

As person A covers he simultaneously strikes out with his left arm, jabbing his fingers into person B's eyes. As a minimum this will ensure that person B moves his head away and will hide A's next attack. Note: A's strike has slipped just over the top of B's arm, and would have been hidden from B's view until the last moment – giving him little chance of retaliating.

Person A now enters and applies an elbow strike into the side of B's ribs with his right elbow.

While moving into person B to strike, A has also withdrawn his left arm to control person B's structure.

Using a coiling motion, this has twisted-up person B's arm and has turned his elbow towards A, coupled with the fact that B's arm is completely straight this now presents a weak point to hit – a good follow up attack from A could be to strike again with the same forearm/elbow technique at the back of B's elbow.

All of the moves shown here are carried out all in one motion, without stopping at all – allowing person A's full body weight to land with his elbow strike against B's ribcage.

Xing Yi - She Xing

She Xing Application 11

This is a classic Yang She Xing movement which seeks to quickly strike the opponent with the side of the fist or the edge of the forearm.

Note: this method can be applied to strike the opponent pretty much anywhere along his flank, including his head/temple area.

Person A attacks B with a high right punch. Person B withdraws slightly (Tui) and covers the attack with his left palm (Tseh) while simultaneously lowering his right arm – B is also storing energy in his body, ready for his strike.

Once person A has moved into a safe position, person B enters and attacks instantly, striking A hard in the side of his ribcage.

Note: this strike is normally delivered with Bright Jin (Ming Jin) energy dynamics - which is like a whip unfurling. However, like all of Xing Yi striking you may also choose to strike using Dark Jin.

She Xing Application 12

Person A attacks B with a high right punch. Person B covers the attack with his left arm while simultaneously moving slightly to his left, this allows B to part-enter, and opens up a clear line of attack for him to follow on his next movement.

Person B now follows-up by instantly entering low and wrapping his arms around A's right (front) leg. Note: you must always be careful when dropping your head down towards an opponent's knee, if the opponent is weighted on his back leg and your timing is wrong, then you are leaving yourself open to getting a knee straight in the face. Therefore good timing is key to entering – in this case Person A has already committed to his attack, and is moving forwards with his weight on his front leg.

After grasping hold of A's leg, B nestles the top of his head into A's stomach and pushes with it, while keeping hold of and lifting his leg. This will give you a small amount of distance, and as you pull the opponent's leg up his body will act like a pivot – enabling you to control him and topple him over.

Note: in true Snake fashion, person B has also trapped A's foot between his legs to control him and straighten out his knee.

Person B turns A while dropping him to the ground. He instantly follows up by dropping his knee into A's stomach and starts to strike.

The photo below shows person B using more control methods as person A tries to escape.

Person B has spread out his weight to give him a firmer and heavier base, while simultaneously pinning down A's left arm, and striking A in the throat with his left forearm. Further strikes and/or control methods will follow.

She Xing Application 12

She Xing Application 13

Person B attacks A with a straight kick using Beng Jin. Person A withdraws (Tui) slightly while blending with the attack and simultaneously slips his left arm under the outside of person B's leg. Note: person A's right arm has also slipped around the inside of B's leg.

Person A now swaps the weight of B's leg onto his right arm, and immediately attacks with the side of his left hand into person B's groin with Pi Jin.

Note: depending on the distance between yourself and your opponent, you may also choose to strike with the edge of your forearm.

It is very hard for person B to defend against this attack as his structure is being completely controlled via his leg.

The strike is also delivered under his leg and therefore completely hidden from his line of sight.

She Xing Application 14

This is the same technique shown in Application 13, but here we can see it being applied differently –with the strike above B's leg and into his ribs.

Person B attacks A with a right kick. Person A withdraws his position while slipping his left arm under person B's leg to control him.

Person A immediately slips his right forearm under B's leg, which frees up his left arm to strike. Person A steps into B's position (enters) while striking into the side of his ribcage with his left forearm/palm. He has also simultaneously raised person B's leg while striking, this creates a pivot point in B's structure and enables person A to 'drive' person B down into the floor.

She Xing Application 15

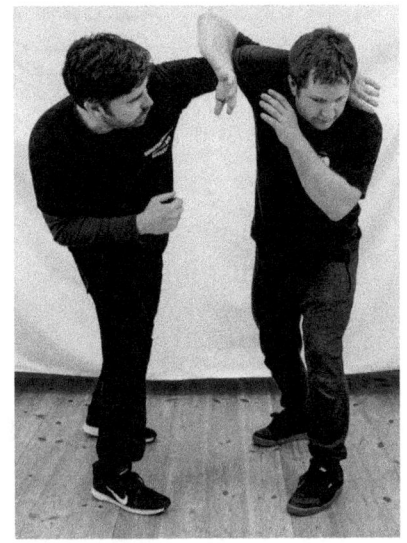

This is a classic She Xing Nui Da method which has been slightly modified here, with Person B carrying out the arm lock while A's left arm is behind his head. Normally A's wrist/arm would be against B's chest, and held there with B's left hand as in 'She Xing Application 1'.

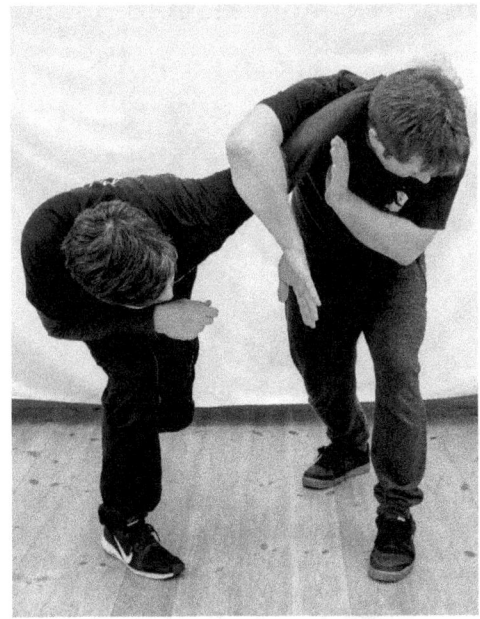

Person A and B have moved in close to each other, and are in a clinch which is turning into a grappling situation.

Person B withdraws his position and turns, while his right arm simultaneously coils around A's left arm – this straightens out A's arm and traps it between B's arm and neck.

Person B's coiling motion continues, and he drops his weight while his right arm points straight down at the floor and also lowers.

Note: this puts a huge amount of force onto A's shoulder and elbow joints, which causes him to drop down and try to escape.

This Yin Snake method has a very heavy/crushing feel to it and if delivered well, not only will you damage your opponents arm joints but you will also be able to control him, while opening up lines of attack to his head or groin for your next strike.

Person B follows up instantly while A is trapped and in pain, with a Pi Jin kick into A's groin area. B's left hand is also ready to strike, so good follow up attacks from here would be to either deliver more kicks to A's groin, or enter with a fist/palm strike to A's head.

She Xing Application 16

Although a great deal of Xing Yi methods are focused on striking with the fists, it is important to practice and use Xing Yi's vast repertoire of leg strikes and kicks.

These are found within all of the Animal Xings and within the Five Elements practice. To a certain extent, kicks in Xing Yi are often hidden within most of the movements.

It is also worth noting that any step which you take in Xing Yi can easily be turned into a kick, even if you are in mid-motion.

Here we see Person A kicking with a Yang She Xing flavour to it, using his kicking leg to dart out and strike the opponent just like the Viper attacking its prey.

This style of kicking allows you to strike whilst maintaining a reasonable amount of distance between yourself and your opponent.

The flavour of this kick is quick and accurate, and your leg/foot also recoils after each strike so as not to be grabbed easily by your opponent – much akin to using quick jabs with your fingers or fists. Prime targets are the groin, knees, and the soft areas inside the opponent's legs.

You can also vary the flavour of the kick by changing its internal dynamics – delivering it by using either Beng, Pi, or Tsuan Jin, or even a combination of Beng and Tsuan Jin together.

She Xing Application 17

Person B attacks A with a straight punch with his right fist.

Person A covers the strike with his left hand/arm and simultaneously slips along the side of the attack (Tseh).

Very little or no pressure has been applied to person B's arm from A, which allows B's attack to keep slipping forwards and will bring person B closer to A (see photo above).

Once in range person A coils high with his right elbow and strikes person B in the face (see photo to the left).

She Xing Application 18

Here we can see another classic She Xing strike which works well against the flank of the opponent's torso, head or arm.

From a compressed and coiled structure, person B has struck out with his right arm using Pi Jin, and in this instance it contacts person A at the side of the armpit. This unbalances person A and disrupts his position, person B will now follow up with more strikes.

Just like all of the movements in Xing Yi, there are many applications that can be derived from them. Therefore this Snake movement could have also been used to strike hard into the flank of the opponent, or if in the right position it can be used to throw the opponent sideways (while trapping their foot or leg with your own).

She Xing Application 19

When striking into the opponent's eyes with She Xing strategy, you either use your fingertips with extended fingers, or the finger joints adjacent to your knuckles, if you form the snake fist as described in an earlier chapter.

The two photos presented here show these two ways of striking into the opponents eyes. It can also be seen that when using the snake formed fist as above, your finger joints will fit nicely into the eye socket of your opponent.

If you have strong/ conditioned hands and are using finger jabs to strike the opponent, this will add and an extra couple of inches to your striking range.

This will prove useful when striking your opponent from slightly further away.

She Xing Application 20

Person B attacks A with a right punch. Person A covers the attack with his left hand while simultaneously flanking along the side of B's arm (Tseh).

At exactly the same time person A strikes up and into B's throat, using the snake formed fist (Quan) with his fingertips bent over.

This attack is very hard to defend against, as A's right hand/arm slips quickly along the inside of B's arm, and will not be seen until the last moment.

Person B is showing the main defence against this attack, which is to try and draw your structure back (Tui) at the last minute, while putting your free hand in the way of the strike.

This may hurt your hand, but it will take a lot of the power away from the strike contacting your throat, chin or eyes.

She Xing Application 21

Person B attacks A with a high right punch. Person A merges with the attack, using his left forearm at the wrist. He proceeds to use Nian Jin to the back of B's arm to slow it down and control his strike, followed by a small amount of Kou Jin to slightly turn B's position.

Person A simultaneously slips his own structure down the side of B's arm, to the point that he has moved almost around the back of B.

He now takes advantage of this position and instantly moves to the back of person B while wrapping both of his arms around him.

Person A drops down and grabs hold of his right wrist with his left hand, and proceeds to compress and squeeze tight using Beng Jin.

Note: before you start to lift, the lower you can get on your opponent the better. This will ensure that their weight will be top heavy, and they will be much easier to throw head first, down to the floor.

You should aim to get below the opponents hips if you can.

Person A now stands up and lifts person B off of the ground. Note: just like the constrictor wrapping around its prey, you must keep body-to-body with your opponent, with no gaps between you at all. If you do this you will find that they are much easier to lift, and it will ensure that they will find it harder to escape from your clinch.

Once person B is off of the ground, person A swings his structure to the left to make person B's feet swing out sideways, while simultaneously dropping B's head towards the floor.

Note: if you are strong enough, a much nastier way of doing this would be for person A to lift his left foot off of the floor and kick person B's feet sideways, this can be followed up by pile-driving B's head into the ground. Remember that if you have picked up your opponent low down (below the hips), the pivot point upon which they will swing sideways is vastly improved, and you will find this pile-drive manoeuvre a lot easier than it sounds.

Take heed when you are practicing this movement, as you can seriously hurt the person being thrown.

In this instance person A follows B down to the floor and drops his knee into him. Person A has also dropped his left arm/hand onto B's shoulder to pin him to the floor – person A proceeds to start striking B with his right fist.

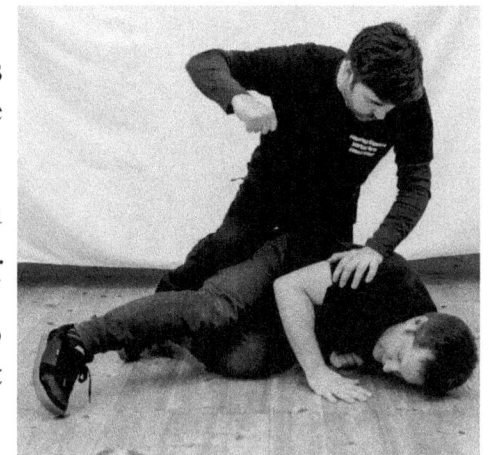

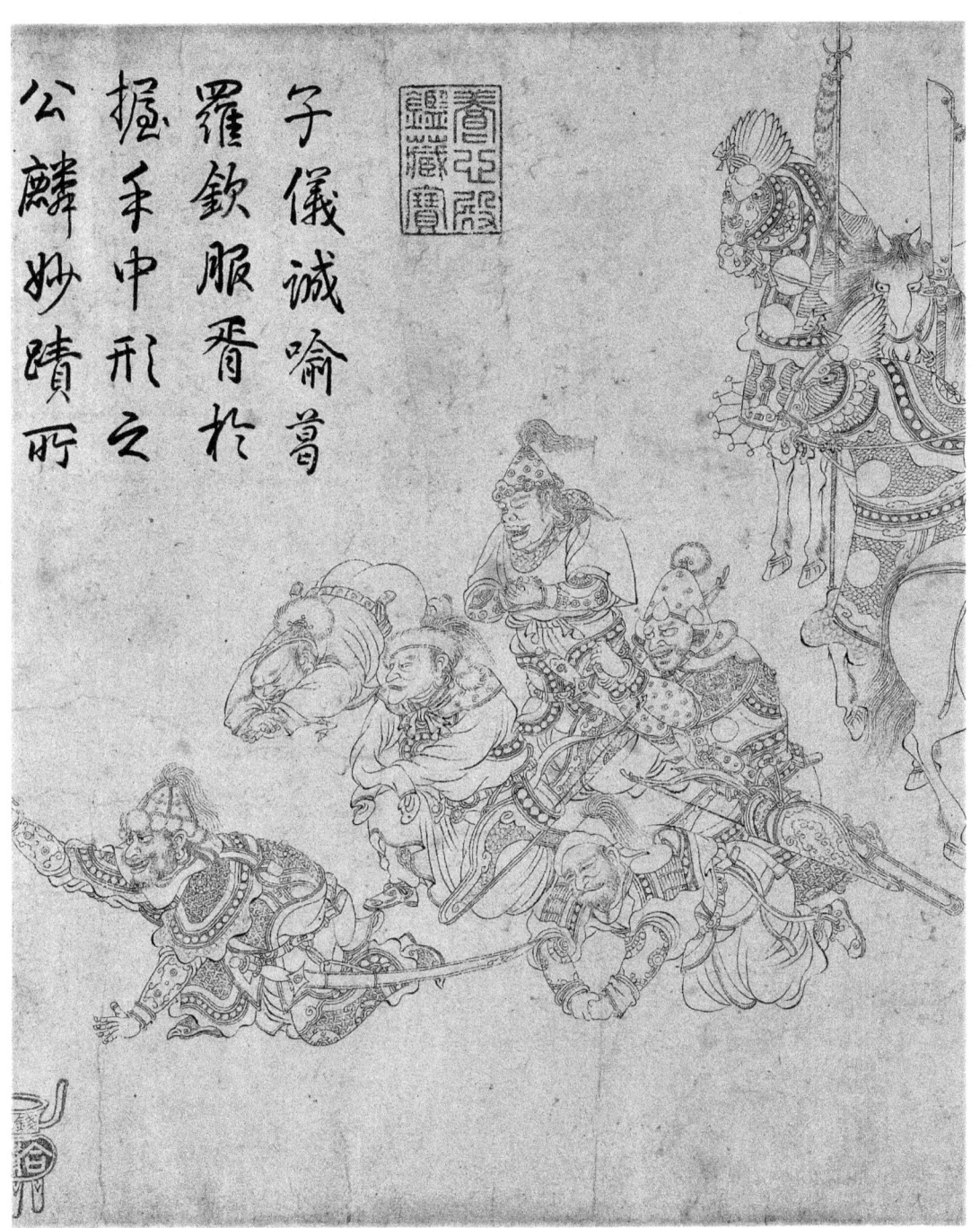

子儀誠喻菖
羅欽服晉於
摳手中形之
公麟妙蹟昕

Lian Huan – Linking Sequence

*'The Outstanding Person Boxes,
Through Freely Releasing Technique...'*

In Xing Yi the term Lian Huan or 'linking sequence' is used to denote the solo practice of 'linking' various physical and energetic structures together. These structures are created when moving with a particular animals Xing, or indeed while moving between postures with the Five Elements Xing Yi practice.

When learning an animal's Xing, your teacher will start by showing you a 'set' linking sequence so that you have something to latch onto, enabling you to pick up the way in which an animal's character moves and acts. These will be the animal's traits which it uses to either defend itself, or hunt its prey.

After practicing a set linking sequence for some time, and having picked up the rudiments of an animals Xing within yourself, it is customary to create your own linking sequences. This is a key stage in your practice so that it does not become stagnant, as the end result which you are aiming for will be to fully embody an animals Xing in combat without forethought.

Once you become proficient in moving with a particular animal Xing, the final stage of this area of your solo practice is to 'free link'. Free linking is when you can naturally move with the character of an animal, without any thought of what move comes next.

You would have now embodied the animal's Xing to the extent that your movements will just happen in the correct way.

At this stage of your practice, the energy dynamics and strategy of the animal which you are using to fight with, will just 'come-out' of you, to flavour all of your movements. This allows you to act spontaneously when in a combat situation, and it is this freedom of thought and movement that will really enable your Xing Yi to be effective.

Over the following pages is presented a short and 'set' Lian Huan sequence for learning She Xing. Like all Lian Huan this is not 'the' She Xing linking sequence, but just a potential way of linking some snake movements together.

A She Xing Linking Sequence

1. Start in San-Ti (formed via Qi-shi) 2/3. Step to your right, simultaneously your left hand rotates high and your right hand moves upwards.

4. Your weight drops down 100% onto your right foot and your body is tightly coiled.

5. Your left foot moves up to meet your right foot (the hand and foot movement all happens at the same time).

6. You strike out to the left, while your left foot enters. The left foot and hand land at the same time. Note: The left hand is striking upwards with Pi Jin while the right hand withdraws. (See Application 1 and 2)

Step to your left, right arm arcing high

Left arm goes up to meet your right arm (as it descends)

Right arm is dropping down with your weight. Left hand covers face

Your right leg 'floats' to meet your left. All weight on your left

Strike out to your right with an upward Pi Jin. Back weighted

Step forwards and slightly right. Right hand goes high. (App 6)

Strike with Beng Jin. (See App 6)

Enter with your right foot while striking with a right Tsuan Chuan

Left leg moving forwards, while right arm rotates to the front

Xing Yi - She Xing

Left leg to front (foot outwards). Hands meet high in front of face

Body coils, right hand drops with body weight. (See Apps 3/8)

Step through with your right leg and strike up with Pi Jin

Turn to your left, spin to the rear and strike with left jab to eyes App 9/10

Variant on last move. Less rotation as opponent is closer

Right foot forward and body weight drops for elbow strike App 10

Turning to your left – next 3 photo's as in App 11

Mid position – body uncoiling to the left

Uncoiled and striking to the left

A She Xing Linking Sequence

 Rotate all the way round to your rear. Left arm covering.	 Facing the rear while striking. The last few pics are all one motion.	 Right hand moving out to strike at eye height
 Right fingers striking, left arm still covering App 9	 Right hand re-coils sharply	 Step through while striking with the left fist using Beng Jin
 Step back to your right. Arms have gone down and moving out and up	 Feet together. Arms have moved up with palms facing inwards	 Arms starting to descend with palms facing down

Xing Yi - She Xing

Your palms have now turned into fists and still moving downwards.

Your fists end up at waist height. As your energy lowers your knees bend slightly.

The final five photos show the traditional way of completing a Lian Huan sequence, if you are finishing your practice then this is the proper way to close it.

Remember that it is important to mix up the movements shown in this short Lian Huan sequence, so that they are linked together in different ways and in a spontaneous manner.

The more spontaneous you can become, the better you will be at embodying an animal's character. Remember to just switch off your thoughts and move with the natural flow of energy that is present.

This is a crucial aspect of your Xing Yi practice - do not get stuck in the trap of moving the same way all of the time with your linking sequences, as this can become detrimental to your progression in the art.

She Xing Weapons - Wu-Bing Fa

*'The Coiling Should Become Tight,
Like the Power that Exists in a Bow at Full Draw...'*

The term Wu-Bing Fa is used in XingYi to denote the use of weapons, and under this umbrella there are a large amount of different concepts and strategies that must be learnt. This includes varying ways of 'forestalling' the opponent, techniques and movements that hinder their movements, and also ways in which you 'borrow' their energy or intent to be used against them. On top of this you will need to become proficient in an array of different skills, many of which are extremely subtle.

A selection of these skills are:

- Body dynamics
- Sensing and 'listening' skills
- Stealth
- Quieting your mind during combat
- Making use of the environment, to combative advantage
- Distance
- Timing
- Creating 'Jins' and applying them appropriately
- Striking with either Dark or Bright Jin
- Energy Dynamics
- Shared Xin
- Strengthening your intention
- Reading your opponents intention
- Flanking
- Simultaneous attack and defence
- Seeing the Heng
- Forestalling methods (Shang Fa)
- Borrowing methods (Jie Fa)

All of these skills are required for both your weapons and bare-hand practice, but during weapons training you will need to really sharpen them, as things tend to move a lot quicker with very little room for error.

Therefore it is essential that your practice incorporates actual two man fighting during your weapons training, so that you can really 'test' if the skills that you have acquired are authentic, and not imagined in any way. It can be said that without learning to use the main weapons in Xing Yi, it would be hard to get to the deeper levels of the art – which is becoming a theme in modern Xing Yi practice, where many of the arts practitioners do no weapons training at all.

Time invested in learning some weapons is well worth the effort, as your bare-hand practice will become sharper and more powerful. So even in the modern world where you are never likely to use weapons for real, there is this pay back as your Xing Yi skills will be far greater, whether you are using a weapon or not.

The bare-hand practice of the art is a more modern addition, and was reputedly started when Grand Master Ji Long Feng (1588-1662) decided to put his weapons to one side and use another way of fighting when he wasn't on the battlefield. The same techniques and fighting skills which were honed through his many hours of armed combat, were now put to good use with his fists and body. In some ways, the areas of the body which are used for striking are viewed as the 'weapons' that are always available to the Xing Yi practitioner. The 'Seven Stars' is a term that you will often hear mentioned, and which denote the main striking areas of the body which are employed to great effect. *Note: see the appendix for a list of the Seven Stars.*

However, it has to be understood that Xing Yi is primarily a weapons art, and the masters of old worked out the most effective animal strategies and methods to use on the battlefield. These were tried and tested over many centuries of battles, during the numerous war campaigns from the Song Dynasty onwards – these battles became the melting  pot that was required, to devise and forge the most destructive and no-nonsense movements for the soldiers.

She Xing strategy is well suited to using most weapons, but a good starting point in your training would be to learn the Spear (Qiang) and straight sword (Jian). Incidentally, spear practice will increase your power and therefore the effectiveness of your striking, and practicing the straight sword will help to sharpen your timing.

The coiling and twisting structures which are created when moving with She Xing are put to good use to control, evade  and strike your opponent from some very unusual angles.

The upwards Pi Jin strike which is so prevalent with She Xing strategy, will ensure that the blade or point of any weapon being used comes into contact with the underside of the opponent.

Prime targets are between the groin, the inside surfaces of the legs (where arteries are located), up into the armpits, and the inside surface of their arms.

Note: This aspect of She Xing was particularly useful for targeting the weak points in the opponents armour when on the battlefield. The mainly concealed areas of the human anatomy are the best places for any armour to be tied, to secure it to its user. These areas are under their armpits, around the groin, and there is also a gap between the helmet and the main body of their armour. This is the reason why many of She Xings striking angles target these areas of the body, so as to easily slip past any armour and into the opponents body. Therefore, She Xing is a fundamental strategy for weapons use.

This low to high strike also has the added advantage of the 'shock-factor', as it is such an unusual angle of attack, which makes it very difficult to defend against if you are not expecting it. Also, this strike is often out of the line of sight of the opponent, which adds a further level to its effectiveness.

When using shorter weapons such as the 'Stings' (Ci/Tsi), these same ascending angles of attack will ensure that the point of the weapon is literally pointing upwards, and therefore can be driven up into the opponents groin, armpit or chin.

Xing Yi's legendary founder, Marshal Yue Fei

Driving the Tsi into the opponents arm or torso, will also enable you to control their position, where you can use the Sting as a handle to hold onto them, and stop them retreating. This will enable you to strike with the other Sting, which will be held in your other hand.

The close range fighting methods of Yin She Xing can be seen when using your weapon to control and 'stick' to the opponents weapon, to hinder and smother their movements. This will enable you to cleverly coil your own weapon around theirs, giving you some very effective striking angles which naturally 'open-up' by adhering to correct technique.

With Yang She Xing strategy, you will be staying at a safe distance which should be gauged so that the opponent's weapon can't reach you. You are seeking to stay just out of range of the opponent's weapon, which will require superior distance and timing skills – this can only be learnt through experience, where you will learn what works for you and what doesn't.

The darting and accurate striking methods that derive from the viper will now come into their own - with patience and by holding your nerve, the opportunities to strike will appear. Do not think about this and just move naturally (with correct Snake Xing strategy), and when the opportunities arise you must strike without forethought. This is the way that Xing Yi works best, no thinking but clear, crisp and natural movements which you are ultimately seeking to be 'driven' by the Xin – and the 'shared Xin' of both participants. As mentioned elsewhere in this book, we call this 'seeing the Heng' in Xing Yi, and this can only occur when in a combat situation.

Yang She Xing methods will seek to quickly strike at the opponent and then withdraw, so you will use your weapon in this manner. The straight sword (Jian) is particularly suited for these fast, darting movements, and as it is such a fast weapon it particularly suits the lithe movements of the viper. You will be able to slip through the gaps in the opponents defence/intent to great effect, enabling your weapon to slip over, or under your opponents weapon or arm.

Using your weapon in this manner will more often than not have an element of stealth to it, as your line of attack will be hidden from their line of sight – utilising the stealth aspect of She Xing.

Weapons training will need to be learnt slowly, with a training partner who is a willing participant. Take your time, and as you both become more proficient you will be able to start speeding up and add deeper levels to your practice.

The An Jin way of delivering strikes really comes into its own with weapons use, as the power of the cut or thrust is 'on' for the duration of any movement. Not only does this help any weapon to go through its target (including armour), but it also has the added advantage of being able to damage the opponent, no matter when the cut or thrust hits them. Thus the depth of range within which the cut of any weapon is under power is large, and if the opponent moves closer or further away they still suffer the same cut.

To finish off, it is worth mentioning that Xing Yi methods instill a 'generalised' weapons sense into the practitioner. This means that with the correct skills, you will be able to use pretty much any weapon which is to hand – irrelevant of the length/weight or size of it.

Of course, certain animal Xings will be better suited to a particular weapon than others, depending on the way in which an animal moves, and the way in which the weapon you are employing is most effective.

The most effective combinations will be explained to you during the transmission from an authentic Xing Yi teacher, there is no other way to learn Xing Yi, and therefore this aspect is crucial. These skills will eventually become 'part of you' during the many hours of practice that will be required, enabling you to learn to use any weapon efficiently and accurately.

She Xing Weapons - Wu-Bing Fa

Appendix

Appendix 1 - The Shenfa (Body Methods)   page 93

Appendix 2 - The Eight Jins of Xing Yi   page 96

Appendix 3 – The Seven Stars   page 101

Appendix 4 - Dark and Bright Jin Striking   page 102

Appendix 5 – Our Xing Yi Lineage   page 104

Appendix 6 – Other Books in this series and information on Xing Yi in the UK   page 105

Appendix 7 – San-Ti Shi (Three Body Posture)   page 108

Appendix 8 – A Comparison of Xing Yi Snake and BJJ   page 114

Graham Barlow takes a brief look at the modern martial art of Brazilian Jiu Jitsu, and how many of its fighting methods have parallels with Yin She Xing.

Although BJJ is a completely different martial art to Xing Yi, I think that this will be of interest to people practicing both arts in the modern world, where BJJ has become very popular and accessible to a large number of people. Graham has practiced Xing Yi for many years and is also a black belt in BJJ, therefore he is well placed to write this short but informative section.

Appendix 1 - The Shenfa

The Shenfa are a group of terms which are usually used by the beginner to intermediate practitioner, and which helps them to understand some of the methods which they are applying,

The Shenfa are as follows:

Di – Which means low or going low. This may refer to the intention or Yi traveling low or descending, and does not necessarily mean that the body is lowered.

Fan – Overturning or reversing. Which has the feel of the energy turning over on itself and coming back in the other direction.

Gau – High or going high. Again this can refer to intention and not just physical movement.

Heng – Crossing. This often is referring to moving sideways and/or crossing the opponent's line of intent. It relates to, but in this context is not the same thing as Heng Jin and Heng Jian/Qiang/Chuan. Although the Chinese character is the same, it is best to consider Heng from the Shenfa separately at first. Another complication can be seen regarding the phrase 'seeing the Heng', which refers to the moment where you see 'the advantage' within the dynamics of a combat situation, we are not referring to this in the Shenfa.

Jin – Entering. Often considered to mean a full forward stepping movement, with the old rear foot becoming the front foot. Technically speaking Jin refers to entering the body into the space which was formerly occupied by the opponent. Thus Jin could also be done with the footwork commonly associated with Zhong (see below). However, this is not referring to the term Jin which is also used to mean combative energy or 'warrior strength'.

Tseh – This is sometimes seen written as 'Ce' and means to flank or 'flanking'. This is the practice of causing the opponent's attack to slide along, just past one's flank without offering any significant resistance to it. Tseh is seen in all of the defensive components of movement in the Five Elements Xing Yi. It is also used in the Animals Xing Yi, but not universally so.

Tui – Withdrawing and/or drawing out. There are a great many different variations on Tui, and these provide a great majority of the more complex footwork used in Xing Yi.

Zhong – Moving straight ahead. A very common method in virtually all of Xing Yi in which the body is moved directly forwards. Typically it is associated with a forward movement without changing the front foot, but it can also be done with the footwork more commonly associated with Jin (see above). The real difference between Zhong and Jin is whether or not one enters the space formerly occupied by the opponent (Jin) or simply advances (Zhong).

At an elementary, though somewhat simplistic level of understanding, Heng, Jin, Zhong and Tui are heavily associated with footwork. While Di, Fan, Gau and Tseh are associated with body dynamics.

An important point to mention, is that the knees should always feel like they 'want to drive forward' and into the opponent. This comes from having a correctly formed San Ti Shi (three body posture), where the chicken leg principle 'urges' the practitioner forward, and each step can therefore become a kick or kick strike at any moment.

Shen literally means 'body' and 'fa' means method. Thus the Shenfa are the basic methods of the body used in Xing Yi. The Shenfa are rarely used in isolation, but rather in simultaneous combinations of two or more.

It is important not to read too much into the Shenfa, as they are not so much underlying principles as they are convenient terms for describing Xing Yi footwork and body dynamics, which help the elementary student to make sense of how their Xing Yi works.

At the intermediate level this understanding is combined with Xing Yi's 'Eight Jins' or ways of creating and using combative energy. It is worth noting here that 'Heng' is common to both the Shenfa and the Eight Jins. This is because of the special/fundamental usage of Heng, which is used to one extent or another in all Xing Yi methods without exception.

Appendix 2 - The Eight Jins of Xing Yi

There are several different words in Chinese that are written as 'Jin' (or Jing) in romanised letters. It is important to note here that when we speak of Jin in Xing Yi, we are not usually talking about the 'Jin' or 'Ching' familiarly associated with Daoism which is roughly translated as 'essence'.

The Jin under discussion here means 'warrior power' or 'combative strength/energy' and has a distinctly militaristic flavour. It relates to the temporal energetic results of condensing or otherwise manipulating the Chi (potential energy) in different ways. In Xing Yi theory, Chi alone does very little, and it must be first condensed into Jin in order to be of practical combative use.

Within each Jin this can be achieved in one of three different ways. The most basic of these is simply to condense the Chi as it flows through the bones, restricting the diameter of its flow in order to increase the power, just as when narrowing the diameter of a hose increases the speed of the water running through it. All eight Jins can be achieved by using this basic way of condensing Chi.

Although the conception of Jin varies slightly from style to style, in our style there are eight fundamental Jins used, seven of which appear in an obvious way in Qishi (which is the formal method of forming San Ti Shi).

Actually the eighth Jin, Beng Jin, also appears within Qishi in a hidden way. The names of the eight Jins are listed in the order that they occur in Qishi, with Beng Jin added at the end, as follows:

1.   *Heng Jin - lit. 'Crossing Jin' or 'Containing Jin'.*

This relates to the energetic results of combined Xin and seeing the Heng. It is the most difficult Jing to grasp because it cannot be produced in isolation from the specifics of any given combative situation. Heng jin is the most fundamental and difficult of the Hsing-I Jins.

It involves joining with the opponent's Chi and leading it in some way such that you create Jin from the opponent's Chi as much as from your own. All Hsing-I methods, without exception, make at least some use of Heng Jin, and Heng Jin is symptomatic of the unification of Hsin, that is, if the Hsin is unified Heng Jin naturally arises. In this sense it is different from the other seven Jins.

2.   *Nian Jin - lit. 'Thread-Making Jin'.*

This is a kind of braking energy that acts partly like a disc break on a car and partly like the energy that a sycamore seed falling makes against the air. Nian Jin is perhaps most clearly seen when a Goshawk takes large prey - it uses spiralling actions against the air to divert and brake the forward momentum of the prey in order to stop it from escaping.

3.   *Kou Jin - lit. 'Hooking Jin'.*

Very much what it sounds like. It relates to hooking power. It is important to note, however that Kou Jin is produced with the whole body, not the arms acting independently.

There is a sense of diverting smoothly while projecting an

unbroken "stream" of Chi. This is akin to fast moving water in a straight pipe suddenly encountering a gradual bend in the pipe.

4. *Tsuan (or Zuan) Jin - lit. 'Drilling Jin' or 'Awling Jin'.*

Drilling Jin is a good translation of this Jin, except that the drilling action of the energy is bi-directional, not mono-directional. Hence the sense of an awl is appropriate.

The movement of the Chi is akin to water spinning inside a pipe as it travels along or like a bullet traveling along a rifled barrel.

Tsuan Jin is used a lot in XingYi to deliver strong upper-cuts to the opponent. It is also useful to combine Tsuan Jin with Beng Jin when punching which will help your strike 'stick' to the opponent on contact and not slip off.

5. *Shun Jin - lit. 'Same Direction Jin'.*

This is combative energy reapplied sharply, and usually immediately, in the same general direction as some previous Jin.

It is a sudden re-reversal, or quick gather into a crashing wave-like action in the same manner or sense that the Chi was previously used an instant before. Exactly how to implement Shun Jin therefore depends upon the Jin used immediately previously.

6. Fan Jin - lit. 'Overturning Jin'.

This is energy that turns or rolls over on itself. With Fan Jin it feels like your energy has been flipped over, just like a pancake. Before the energy 'turns over' there is also a shudden 'fullness' to the experience of this Jin. A bit like a balloon inflating.

Once it has flipped over, the energy continues to move in the new direction that has been created. This often works well in combination with Pi Jin, i.e. after the energy has turned (often downwards) you strike using Pi Jin.

7. Pi Jin - lit. 'Splitting Jin'.

Probably the most famous Jin in Xing Yi. This is like the action of an axe or cleaver chopping through and splitting wood. It is the acceleration (and, in more advanced methods, also deceleration) of the Chi (Not physical acceleration).

Traditionally described as "rise and fall", but this does not mean in a vertical direction, but rather more like "accelerate and decelerate" (i.e. rising and falling in time). The action of the Chi is like the flow of water intermittently speeding up and slowing down.

8. Beng Jin - lit. 'Holding a Bow at Full Draw Jin'.

This arises naturally from the expansion and contraction of the Chi in the whole body, and is probably the most basic Jin in Xing Yi. Beng Jin is useful in adding power to strikes in either its expansive (Yang) or contractive (Yin) phases.

Another important use of Beng Jin is to protect your body against heavy incoming strikes. When contracting the Chi of the body into the organs a tight and strong structure is created which stops the energy from your opponent's strikes penetrating your deeper tissues and keeping you safe. In some ways this is looked at as Xing Yi's very own 'iron shirt' training which creates a very 'dense' feeling within the body, while on the surface it still remains light and soft.

In addition to the above eight Jins there are other named Jins, such as Tsun Jin (Inch Jin), however these are simply specialised applications of the other eight. For instance Tsun Jin (also written Cun Jin) is a specialised application of either Beng Jin or Shun Jin, depending on how it is done.

Appendix 3 – The Seven Stars

Striking in Xing Yi can be delivered with any part of the body, limbs or head, and Jin can be created and transmitted in to the opponent through any of these. The 'Seven Stars' is a phrase which is often used in Xing Yi to denote the main areas of the human anatomy which are used for striking, and these are:

- Elbows
- Head
- Shoulders
- Hands
- Feet
- Knees
- Hips

The areas of the body listed above are viewed as 'the weapons' that are always available to the Xing Yi adept, and they also serve to give a flavour of the Xing Yi fighters world view regarding his barehanded practice – where he often views his own body as a weapon.

The list is not exhaustive as there are other areas of the body used, for example, using the sides of the forearms to strike the opponent when fighting with Tuo Xing (Crocodile).

Appendix 4 - Dark and Bright Jin Striking

Broadly speaking the eight fundamental categories of Jin can be applied in one of two ways, these being:

- Dark Jin (An Jin – also sometimes termed Hei Jin)
- Bright Jin (Ming Jin)

When striking, the application of 'Bright Jin' has an exponential power curve, and the strike happens when the energy is at its highest point. This is a bit like the energy that is applied when using a whip, where with correct timing, the last unfurling of the whip will transmit the highest amount of energy into the target being struck. The Shanxi braches of Xing Yi tend to favour this way of striking.

As already mentioned, our school of Xing Yi was handed down to us via three different lineages which are all descended from Mater Guo Yun Shen of Hebei Province. The term 'Hebei Xing Yi' can be used to categorise lineages which have all descended from Master Guo, who lived and taught Xing Yi for many decades in this province of China.

Hebei style Xing Yi, or 'Old Hebei Style' as it is sometimes called (this is to differentiate it away from the modern and 'watered down' WuShu Hebei Styles) favours the piercing 'Dark Jin' (or An Jin) striking which was particularly useful in penetrating armour with weapons.

In unarmed combat this type of striking is also extremely effective as the strike on contact does not decelerate, but instead carries on 'through' the opponent - no matter where they are struck.

This type of striking causes maximum damage to the opponent, and the constant displacing/disruption of their position will also hinder them from becoming composed again. This is completely different to a push where the power diminishes on contacting the target, and then accelerates again to 'push' the person away.

If you have never experienced this type of striking before, it is somewhat difficult to explain how to do it in a book. Instead it requires the person learning Dark Jin striking to be struck with it, so that he can feel the energetic quality being used. He can then learn how to replicate the same dynamics for himself, while striking his training partners in a controlled way during practice.

Dark Jin has a 'piercing' feeling to it, and will displace the opponent's body mass as the strike goes through them, without slowing down in the slightest. Just as an Eagle 'punches through' its prey with its strong talons. As such Dark Jin has a constant power profile as opposed to the exponential power curve as seen with Bright Jin striking.

Even within our Hebei descended school of Xing Yi, some of the animals will have 'Brighter' strikes than others, so it can be seen that the differing 'flavours' of the animal characters have their unique ways of striking and power generation.

Needless to say, it doesn't matter if you are practicing branches of the art from Hebei or Shanxi provinces, or striking with Bright or Dark Jin, as long as you are adhering to the fundamental principles and strategies of the art, then you are most definitely using Xing Yi.

Appendix 5 – Our Xing Yi Lineage

The Xing Yi in our lineage passes through three different lines down to my teacher, and all three of them came through Master Guo Yun Shen. One of these lineages can be shown as:

1. Ji Long Feng
2. Cao Ji Wu
3. Dai Long Bang
4. Li Neng Ran
5. Guo Yun Shen
6. Liu Chi Lan
7. Li Cun Yi
8. Hao En Guang
9. Luo Da Cheng
10. Zhu Guang
11. Damon Smith
12. The Author

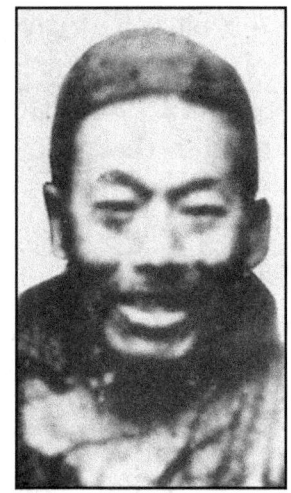

Master Guo Yun Shen

The other two lines which have been transmitted to my teacher have come to us via traditional Xing Yi family styles, and which have fortunately, completely bypassed the modern influence of Wu Shu. However at the request of my teacher, the other two lines of Xing Yi in our lineage will remain private.

Appendix 6 – Other Books in this Series and Information on Xing Yi in the UK

Xing Yi Bear Eagle: this is the first book in this series and was written by my Xing Yi teacher. This is an excellent book which makes an in depth study of this fundamental Xing. There are also sections on spear, needles and sword methods.

Damon Smith, Jeremy Mills Publishing 2004.

Xing Yi Tai and Tuo Xing: this book takes a look into the fascinating fighting strategies of two of the less well known animals within Xing Yi. The book also covers many other areas of the art, much of which has not been released before in English books on the subject.

Xing Yi Groups in the UK

If you are in the UK and are looking to learn Xing Yi, then please contact one of the following groups. *(Note: there are other groups, but these are the ones that I am personally associated with)*

Xing Yi in Cornwall, Somerset and Devon:

Please take a look at our website: xingyi.org.uk if you are looking to learn Xing Yi in the South West of the UK.

Yongquan Martial Arts Association:

They have a website which will enable you to look for teachers that are located throughout the UK. You will be able to find tuition in the following martial arts:

- Old Hebei Xing Yi
- Tai Chi Chuan
- Buk Sing Choy Li Fut

FoXfist:

If you are interested in learning and practicing a variety of martial arts, and are located in the South West of England, then have a look at FoXfist.

Their website is www.foxfist.com where you will also be able to find their contact details. They practice a variety of martial arts which include Xing Yi, and like to experiment and cross train with these.

Some of the martial arts covered are: Baji Quan, Xing Yi, Traditional Kempo, Bak Sing Choy Li Fut, Dorjee Lam, Brazilian Jiu-jitsu and Plum Flower Boxing.

All of the groups listed above are traditional, and are therefore non-profit making.

Mike Ash, practicing some She Xing methods

Appendix 7 San Ti Shi - Three Body posture

'Internal and External, front and rear, are combined, This is called 'Threading into One...'

San Ti Shi, or 'three body posture' is Xing Yi's way of creating very strong, mutually supportive structures in the body of the practitioner.

Although hard to see with the untrained eye, many circles and triangles are created in and around the body due to the structure of three body posture, giving it incredible strength. It is well known that circles and triangles are some of the strongest structural shapes that we know of, and engineers have always made use of their properties. The circles and triangles created are not just in the physical body, but are also within the connections of the energy inside and surrounding you.

An example of this can be seen in the triangles between the ankle, knee and hip of the supporting leg, or between the hand, elbow and shoulder on each arm. Of course there are many examples in the body's chi and structure, which are beyond the scope of a book, but as you become more familiar with San Ti Shi you will find many more of these three fold structures.

The Kua is held closed when in San Ti, and the weight is held on one leg which is very different to what we see in most other internal styles. One of the benefits of closing the inguinal crease (Kua) is to keep the knees close together, which aids as a defence for any low kicks to the groin.

After gaining some experience of San Ti Shi, your chi will start to feel very strong and the energy which surrounds you will take on the shape of a large sphere. This spherical or 'chalice like' feeling of your energy, not only adds great integral strength to your structure, but will add to your striking power, and will also act like a barrier – aiding your defence. *(Note: This sensation is part of what is sometimes termed Xin Ding Shen Ning in Xing Yi)*

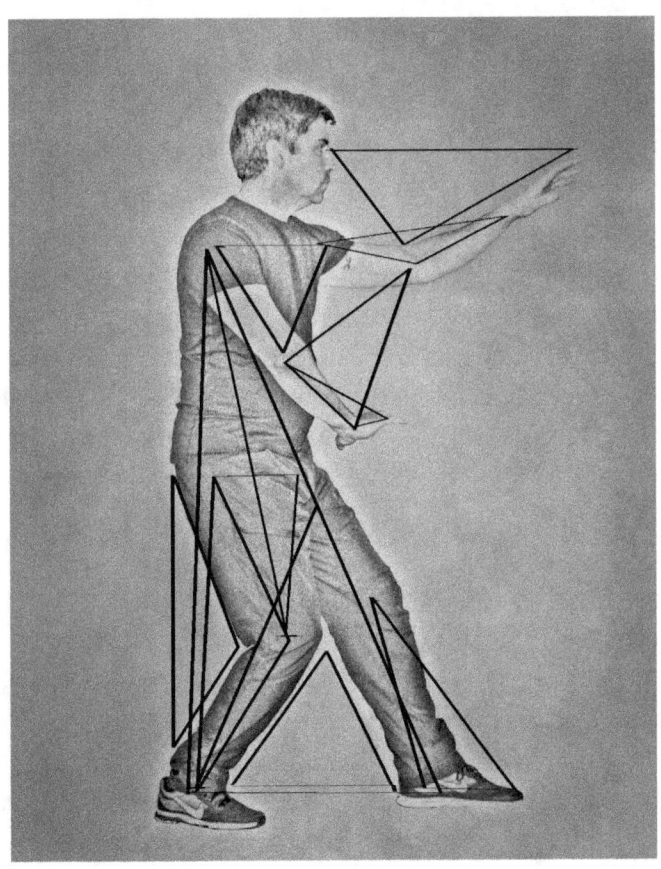

In creating the three body posture, it is crucial that you embody the following principles:

Bear Shoulders

Dragon Waist (Body)

Tiger Embrace

Eagle Claw

Chicken Leg

Thunder Sound

These six principles are key to the formation of San Ti Shi, and therefore key to the formation of all of your physical and energetic structures, which will be created throughout your study of all of the animal Xings.

The Six Principles:

Bear Shoulders – This refers to the way in which the shoulders are 'rounded' and the chest is hollowed, to increase structural integrity. This significantly increases the strength of your structure when striking through your opponent.

Dragon Waist or 'Dragon Body' – When you get a grasp of this feeling in the body, it allows you to generate power through torsion from the waist, rather than through turning the hips. Dragon Body therefore allows the Xing Yi adept to deliver heavy strikes fluidly and constantly, without there ever being a 'stop' in the flow of energy. A useful skill to have which is not seen in many other martial arts, where the energy often comes to a stop at the end of a strike, allowing a 'gap' which the opponent can slip into and attack.

Tiger Embrace – This is the feeling of having a rounded structure, somewhat akin to holding a large ball in front of you.

Eagle Claw – This is the principle that the nails are bowed inwards, that is, the palms of the hands are hollowed and form claws, and the toes claw the ground. When using a weapon it is no different, just that the weapon is seen as a natural extension of the Eagle Claws. The key point is that in applying the principle of Eagle Claw, the Chi at the nail endings becomes 'full'.

Chicken Leg – This is what gives Xing Yi its famous footwork, which is not seen in any other martial art. The supporting leg holds and moves the practitioner along the ground like that of a fighting Cockerel. Depending on the application, the other leg will have a slight amount of weight held on it or none at all. This principle gives Xing Yi footwork its unique 'flavour', and makes it extremely agile in application.

Thunder Sound – This principle is referring to the sound made when striking without an opponent in front of you. When moving and striking correctly, and adhering to the other five principles listed above, then the energy of the strike makes a 'sound like thunder' when your feet make contact with the ground. This concept gives the particular 'flavour' to the strikes in Xing Yi. When striking an opponent, the 'thunder sound' is not heard as the energy will be delivered cleanly into them and not into the ground.

All of the structures which are created throughout the whole of Xing Yi will adhere to these principles, and therefore will be adhering to the three-fold principles of San Ti Shi on many levels (both physically and energetically).

Also, when your weight has been placed onto the front leg, then this is still San Ti. But, for strategic reasons you have decided to withdraw your 'normally seen' front leg to the rear (i.e. the non-load bearing leg at the front has been held at the rear).

The structure of San Ti Shi allows the Chi to permeate throughout all of the tissues of the body cleanly and without any obstruction. It also allows the body to store up a reserve of chi ready for immediate use. In one sense the whole body becomes a chi reservoir. But by itself the Chi has relatively little combative value, but you must learn to control and manipulate it in order to create Jin (combative strength).

There is a famous saying in Xing Yi which states:

'There is nothing but structure and nothing but Chi'

When you have embraced the principles of San Ti, then you can really start to understand what this statement means, as this fundamental aspect of Xing Yi will permeate throughout your practice.

Mike Ash practicing Yin She Xing

A comparison of Xing Yi Snake and BJJ
by Graham Barlow

"In the fight, only one person can be comfortable. Your job is to transfer the comfortable from your opponent to you."

(Rickson Gracie)

Whilst it favours striking, Xing Yi also contains many grappling methods, known as Niu Da, amongst its animals, particularly Snake.

As a black belt in Brazilian Jiu-Jitsu (BJJ) and also a practitioner of Xing Yi, I've always been aware of the similarity between the choking and locking methods of BJJ and Xing Yi Snake. In one sense, you can look at all of BJJ as Xing Yi Snake applied in a grappling situation.

Brazil is, of course, home to some of the largest snakes on earth, and you have to wonder how much influence the impressively large anacondas and boa constrictors of the Amazon have had on the Brazilian style of Jiu-Jitsu.

Imported from Japan by a student of Kan Jigor, called

Mitsuyo Maeda and taught to the Gracie family, BJJ is a unique style of Jiu-Jitsu that emphasises live sparring (called rolling) and practicality over tradition. It is considered a fundamental component of modern Mixed Martial Arts (MMA) due to its efficiency.

BJJ is unusual in that it is both a sport and a martial art at the same time, and as such it is continually evolving. New techniques are discovered, or rediscovered, all the time and rise or fall in popularity due to their success in competition alone.

The following pages contain the BJJ techniques which I think best exemplify the principles of Xing Yi Snake in action. I have included them here because I think that re-examining these techniques with one eye on the principles behind them might help a Xing Yi practitioner gain some insight into applying Xing Yi Snake in a wider context. Xing Yi practitioners might object to the presence of BJJ techniques in a Xing Yi book, but my teachers have always encouraged me to try other martial arts, and I believe that there is much to be gained by comparison with other arts.

Application 1: Rear Naked Choke

While the technique presented here is a basic Rear Naked Choke it's important to note that the flavour of Xing Yi Snake is being employed throughout. Your arm literally snakes under the opponent's chin until you can grab your own bicep and apply the heavy pressure, which is so characteristic of the boa constrictor.

i) B controls A's left hand chin. at the wrist.

ii) B snakes his arm under A's

iii) B grasps A's shoulder to secure his position.

iv) A places his palm on top of his other hand.

v) B slides his arm behind A's and prepares to squeeze.

vi) B grasps his own bicep and Constricts his whole body, completing the blood choke.

Application 2: Snake wrist lock vs collar grab

This application uses the classic Snake arm and wrist Niu Da technique shown elsewhere in this book, but this time from a same-side collar grab. Collar grabs are a frequent occurrence in the stand-up portion of a BJJ match, so this is a common situation, and the twisting Snake lock is an excellent counter that can take your opponent by surprise.

i) A takes a grip on B's collar.

ii) B latches on to A's wrist.

iii) B starts to twist A's arm.

iv) B press his arm downwards, dropping his body weight.

v) B completes the move, bringing A heavily to the ground. A's arm should be completely locked at both the wrist and forearm, ready for a joint break, securing the submission.

Application 3: Fireman's Carry vs collar grip

From the same collar grip you can also enter into throwing techniques. The Fireman's Carry is a popular wrestling technique and this particular entry shares a lot in common with the wrapping and coiling techniques of Xing Yi Snake, and also the switching from high to low that is characteristic of the animal.

i) A takes a grip on B's collar.

ii) B latches on to A's sleeve.

iii) B starts to coil under A's arm. and begins lowering his position.

iv) B drops low and underhook's A's leg, drawing everything in.

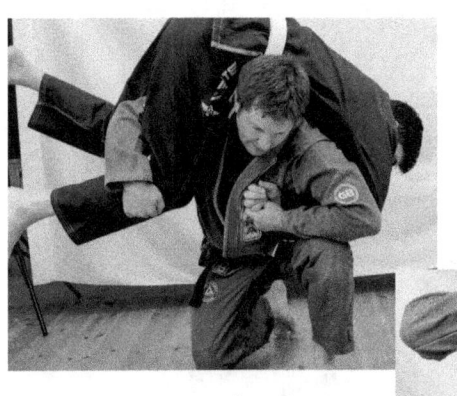

v) B raises up and twists to his right, which has the effect of throwing A over his shoulders.

Xing Yi - She Xing

Application 4: Double Leg

The Double Leg is a popular technique in all types of grappling where grabbing the legs is permitted, but it's interesting to analyse it in terms of Xing Yi Snake's preference for going low then high. It incorporates several of the Xing Yi Shen Fa (body methods): Zhong, "entering", Di, "go low" and Gau, "go high".

i) B proactively separates A's arms, ready for a shot.

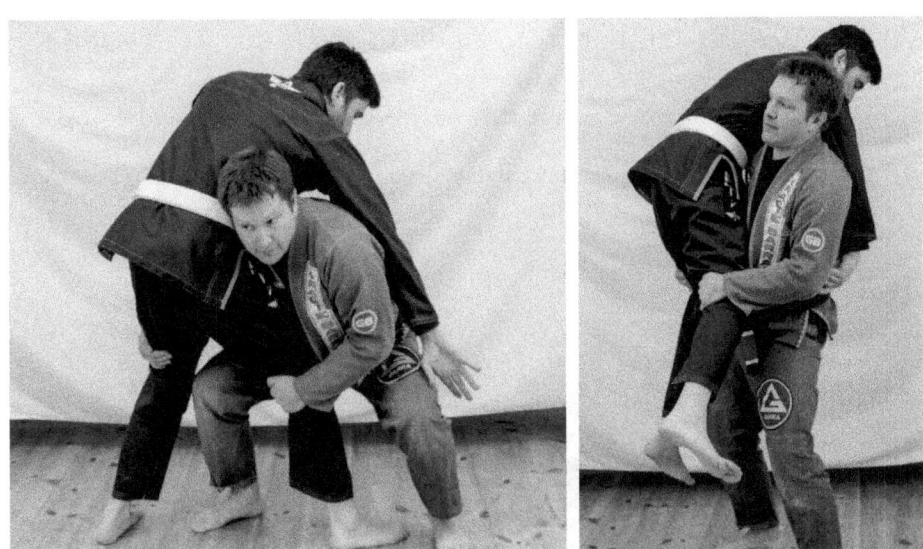

ii) B enters using Zhong and goes low (Di), then goes high (Gau).

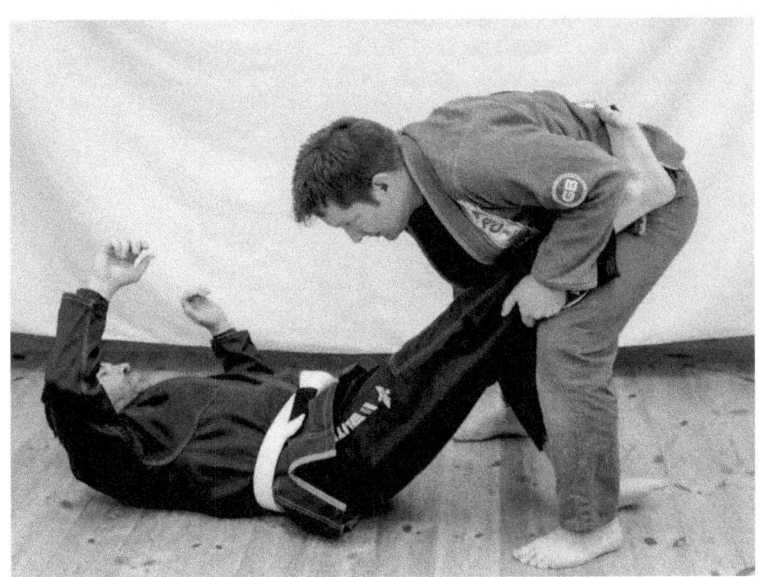

iii) B drops A on the floor and is ready to advance his position.

Xing Yi - She Xing

Application 5: Armbar from open guard

This application again uses heavy constriction to wrap-up an arm and lock it at the elbow joint. Even on the ground, the hand positions are very similar to Xing Yi Snake.

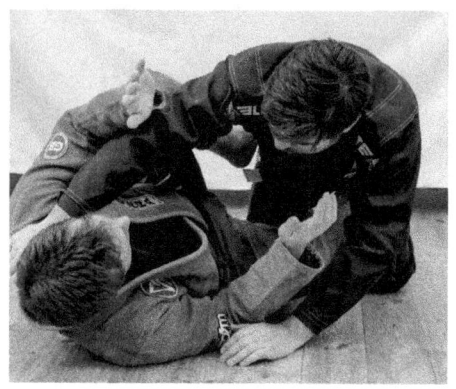 

i) B is in A's open guard, with feet on the hips. ii) A wraps an arm.

iii) A continues with heavy, constriction on the arm, adding in his knee to the back of B's shoulder to achieve an elbow lock.

Application 6: Arm drag to the back

Getting to your opponent's back with an arm drag utilises wrapping and coiling, then the takedown uses Gau "go high" and Di "go low" in quick succession.

i) A secures a 2 on 1 grip on B's arm.

ii) A moves to B's back.

iii) A raises B up.

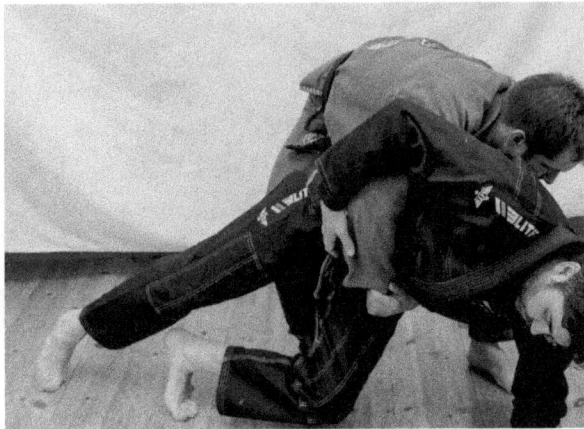

iv) A drops B and continues his attack.

Application 7: Leg entanglements (Ashi Garami)

The idea of wrapping and coiling from Snake is exhibited perfectly in the BJJ leg lock game, where your legs snake around the opponent's as you try to isolate their foot.

i) Starting in the Ashi Garami (Leg entanglement) position, A has his foot on B's hip.

ii) A switches to a modified X Guard position and starts to reach for B's foot and knee.

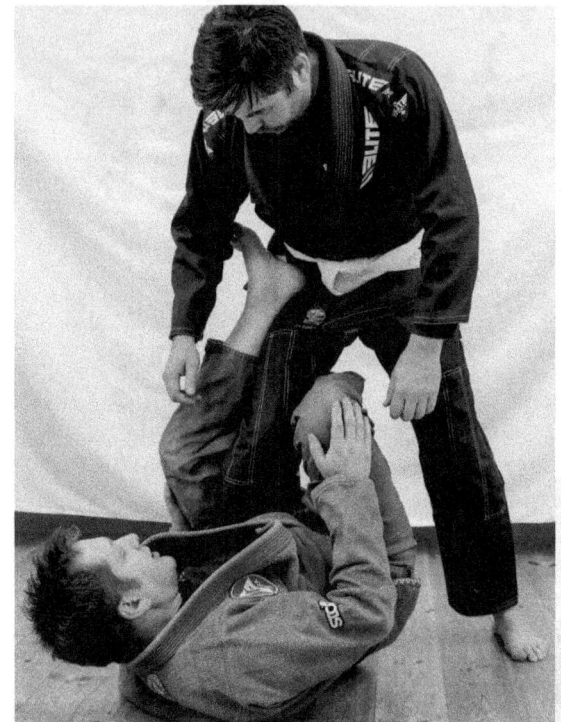

iii) A pulls on B's knee, kicks his other leg and takes him to the ground.

iv) A replaces his foot on B's hip to secure the position.

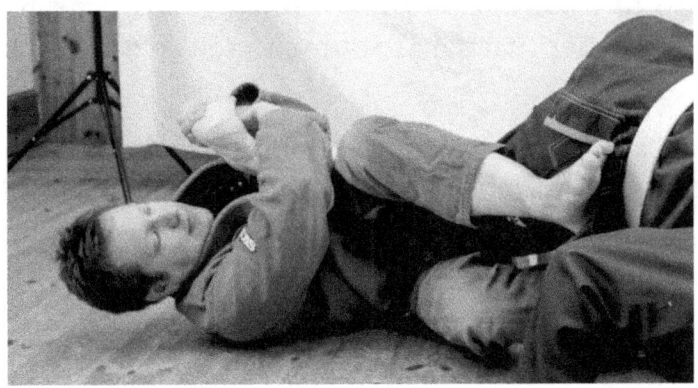

v) With the position secure, A reaches for a toe hold to obtain the submission.

About the Author

The author has been studying martial arts since 1985, and started when he was 12 years old. During the first 8 years of his practice he studied and taught a variety of fighting arts which included Western Boxing, Karate, Hung Gar, Wu Style Tai Chi Chuan and Wing Chun.

It was in 1988 that he first heard of the Chinese Internal Arts (Nei Jia) and was fascinated in learning more about them. Especially Xing Yi, where the stories of its masters with their fighting prowess fascinated him.

At the age of 19 he started training in another fascinating and rare martial system which has a no-nonsense outlook to combat, and with its origins deeply intertwined with the religious systems of Tibet.

Dorjee Lam or the 'Thunderbolt Path' now became his main practice for close to a decade, although during this time he was also practicing other martial arts which included Ba Gua Zhang.

Eventually, in 2002 he was fortunate enough to find an authentic Xing Yi teacher after meeting Sifu Damon Smith. This meeting left a lasting impression on him and following a traditional 'interview' he at last began to learn traditional Hebei Xing Yi Quan.

Since 2002 he has devoted his practice to Xing Yi, although during this time he has also been lucky enough to learn and practice some other rare arts including - Baji Quan, traditional Kempo and Buk Sing Choy Li Fut. He is also an instructor with the Yongquan Martial Arts Association.

國立故宮博物院藏品

Glossary

In this book, a simplified version of the Pin Yin system of romanisation has been used, except in cases where a particular term is either more familiar in the Wade-Giles romanisation, or else where the Pin Yin romanisation is particularly misleading regarding pronunciation. While this method is not very rigorous, it is hoped that it will lead to a greater ease of identification of the terms used.

An Jin/Jing	'Dark Jin' combative energy – also see Hei Jin.
An Shen Pao	A famous two-man linking sequence Literally "Safe Body Cannon" or "Stable Body Cannon".
Ba	The part of the bow held when shooting.
Beng Gong	Bow drawn to the full.
Beng Jian	Bow drawing sword.
Beng Qiang	Bow drawing spear.

Beng Quan	Bow drawing fist.
Bi	Weapon shaped like a writing brush.
Bingfa	Strategy.
Bingqi	Battlefield weapons.
Cao Ji Wu	(c.1670-1770) - A famous Xing Yi master and the senior (known) student of Master Ji Long Feng.
Ce	See Tseh.
Chan	Enwrapping/binding.
Chan	Sparrowhawk. See Yao.
Cheng Xin	Make the Xin clear/transparent.
Che Ti Zhai	(1831-1912) - A famous Xing Yi master who was the top student of Master Li Neng Ran. Master Che's best student was his friend Master Guo Yun Shen.
Chi	Natural energy. In Xing Yi the term generally refers to potential energy that becomes expressed power in the form of Jing.
Chi	Sheath for the head of a spear or lance.
Chia	A type of lance.

Chin Na	See Niu Da.
Chiyi	Put away one's weapons after a combat. Literally "fold the wings".
Chou	(or Toukui) Helmet.
Choujin	Cut the backs of the ankles.
Chuan	See Quan.
Dao	Broadsword/Sabre. Literally "blade".
Daoren	The cutting edge (of a bladed weapon).
Di	Literally "low". One of the Shen Fa.
Di Fa	See Di.
Dun	Shield.
Fan	Overturning/Reversing. One of the Shen Fa.
Fanghu	Gauntlet.
Fan Jing	Overturning power.
Feng	(Head) butt.
Fu	That part of the armour protecting the legs and/or knees.
Fuyue	A category of Chinese battlefield weapons comprising halberds, battle-axes, axe-like halberds and similar. There exist a bewildering variety of such weapons, hence the general classification.

Gan	Pronged metal rod (this is the ancestor of the Okinawan Sai made famous through Okinawan Kobudo and Karate).
Gau	Literally "high". One of the Shen Fa.
Gau Fa	See Gau.
Gong Xian	Bow string.
Gongtou	*The tips (ends) of* a bow.
Gong Xian	Bow string.
Gou	The cord binding on a sword hilt.
Gui	Turtle.
Gui Xing	Character of the Turtle.
Gunn	Staff.
Guo Yun Shen	(1839-1911) - A famous Xing Yi master. Student of Master Li Neng Ran. He was Master Li's second best student and Guo also studied extensively under Master Li's best student Master Che Ti Zhai.
Hanjia	Armour in a physical rather than usage sense. That which is produced by a Hanren or armourer.
Heijing	Dark Jing (also termed An Jin)

Heng	Crossing. One of the Shen Fa. In another sense, control of the opponent's position in general.
Heng Jian	Crossing Sword.
Heng Jing	Crossing/containing/controlling power.
Heng Qiang	Crossing Spear.
Heng Quan	Crossing Fist.
Hou	Monkey.
Hou Xing	Character of the Monkey.
Hu	Tiger. Panthera tigris amoyensis, the so called South Chinese Tiger.
Huan Jiachou	The method of donning armour. See Jiachou.
Hubao	Tiger Embrace.
Hui Shen	The characteristic circular turns used in Xing Yi.
Hu Xing	Character of the Tiger.
Ji	Chicken.
Ji	Gather/accumulate.
Jiachou	(or Kuijia) Armour.
Jian	Straight, double edged sword.
Jian	Arrow.

Jianbing	Hilt of the sword.
Jianfeng	The point of a sword.
Jian Shu	Sword Arts.
Jian Xiao	Scabbard of a sword.
Jiaofeng	Exchange the points of weapons. Roughly the same meaning as Jiaoshou.
Jiaoshou	Exchange of techniques, i.e. fighting.
Jibu	Literally "Fast Step". Often, but not always, a variant of Zhong or Jin in which the body is extended forwards rapidly to attack. In the Bear Eagle this kind of stepping is often used in conjunction with the Yang variant posture.

Ji Long Feng (1620-c.1720) - The historical founder of Xing Yi. He was also known as Ji Ji Ke. He is thought to have taught two famous students, Master Cao Ji Wu and Master Ma Xue Li. In an alternative history the link to Master Ma Xue Li is removed by one generation and there is a story that he was taught by an unnamed person (possibly Cao Ji Wu). Another theory is that there were two men called Ma Xue Li, who were father and son, which is said to have clouded the historical situation.

Jian Kong Bu Da, Jian Heng Da – Literally, "See/catch an opening do not strike, see/catch the Heng strike". A fundamental strategic principle in Xing Yi.

Jie Fa — Literally, "Borrowing Methods". A broad classification of methods in which the opponent's intention (Yi) is "borrowed" in defence. Considered to be the easier way to use Xing Yi methods compared to the more advanced Shang Fa.

Ji Ji Ke — Another name for Ji Long Feng.

Jiju — See Ji (2).

Jin — Entering. One of the Shen Fa.

Jing — Power. Literally "warrior strength". Generated by transformation of the Chi using one or more of several methods.

Jitui — Chicken leg.

Ji Xing — Character of the Chicken.

Jueshi	Archer's thumb ring.
Jue Xian	Draw the bowstring. See Lagong.
Junbing	Battlefield weapons (i.e. not civilian weapons). Also refers to soldiers/things military in general. See also Bingqi.
Kai	Mail (armour component).
Kan	The shaft of a spear.
Kou Jing	Hooking power.
Kuo	Bow at full draw.
Lagong	Bow drawing actions common in Xing Yi methods.
Lan	Bow case.
Li	(In this context combative) advantage.
Lian Huan	Linking sequence (i.e. not a form).

Li Neng Ran (1807-1888) - A famous Xing Yi master who was also known as Li Luo Neng. He almost certainly learned Xing Yi from Master Dai Long Bang, who in turn learned from Master Cao Ji Wu, a student of Grandmaster Ji Long Feng. Master Li went on to teach several very famous masters including Master Che Ti Zhai,

	Master Guo Yun Shen, Master Zong Shi Rong, and Master Li Zhen Bang.
Linjia	Literally "scales-armour". A collective term for the various components that make up the armour.
Liu	Battleaxe.
Liu He	Six Combinations.
Long	Dragon.
Long Xing	Character of the Dragon (the character of Homo sapiens when at their most noble in spirit).
Luo Shi	A name literally meaning simultaneously "Leave Behind Posture" and "Swooping Posture".
Luo Xing Quan	– "Conch Shell Shaped Fist". A basic method of forming the fist both for holding a weapon and for punching in Xing Yi.
Ma	Horse
Ma Di Quan	– Horse's Hoof Fist.
Mao	A basic long spear or lance such as was used to arm irregulars.

Ma Xing — Character of the Horse.

Ma Xue Li (1714–1790) - there may have been two men called Ma Xue Li, possibly father and son. In this case the dates that we have are for the younger of the two men. In tradition he was the other well known student of Ji Long Feng, although there is a chance it was actually Cao Ji Wu or another of Ji Long Feng's students who he learned from most.

Mingjing — Bright Jing.

Nian Jing — Thread making power.

Niu Da — Grappling to obtain position (rather than for its own sake). This is perhaps a better term to describe the strategic use of grappling methods in Xing Yi compared to the more familiar term Chin Na.

Pao Jian — Cannon Sword.

Pao Qiang — Cannon Spear.

Pao Quan — Cannon Fist.

Pi — Split.

Piao — The point of a sword or spear.

Pi Jian — Splitting Sword.

Pi Jing	Splitting power.
Pi Qiang	Splitting Spear.
Pi Quan	Splitting Fist.
Qi	Pin Yin for Chi.
Qi Shi	Literally "starting posture", or "moving posture".
Qi Shi	Used in another sense, Qi Shi refers to the formal and semi formal patterns used in the formation of San Ti Shi prior to practice.
Qi Yu Li He	- The principle that the Chi combines with the strength. See Xin Yu Yi He for discussion of multiple meanings of "Yu".
Qiang	Spear.
Qixie	Weapons in the sense of "the tools of Xing Yi"
Quan	Boxing/Fist/Martial Arts
San Ti	The Three Bodies (the phases applicable in one sense to Heaven, Earth and Man; that is, the Creative, the Receptive and the Manifest)

San Ti Shi	Three Body Posture.
Shang Fa	Literally, "Forging Ahead Methods". A more advanced way to use Xing Yi than Jie Fa. In Shang Fa the opponent's intention (Yi) is forestalled in one of several ways.
Shao	The ends of the bow.
She	Snake.
She	Archer's thumb ring.
Shegou	Archer's arm guard.
Shen	God. Sometimes translated as "spirit", but this is misleading because one of the areas in which Xing Yi differs from some branches of Daoism is in the conception of Shen. Xing Yi was developed by soldiers, not monks, so the meaning of Shen is closer to that found in Chinese folk religion. The sense here is of the dynamic essence underlying nature, which constitutes the ancient popular conception of God in China.
Shen Fa	Body methods.

Shen Gu Di Xing – Literally, "Attend to the Shape of the Ground". The skills of making strategic use of terrain in Xing Yi.

She Xing   Character of the Snake.

Shi   Pattern/structure/posture/style.

Shi Er Xing Jiaoshou – Twelve Characters Fighting (usually translated as "Twelve Animals Fighting").

Shun Jing   Same direction power.

Shuo   A very long lance (some as much as 20ft in length).

Sichao   The universal Xin. The "thoughts" of God within Nature.

Tai   The Flycatcher. *Terpsiphone paradisi.*

Tai Xing   Character of the Flycatcher.

Tai Xing Quan – The way of forming the fist for striking while using Tai Xing. The knuckle of the middle finger being extended.

Taiyi   Another name for Zhongnan Mountain. See Zhongnan.

Ti   Whetstone.

Tian   Heaven. The Creative.

Tiekai	A coat of mail.
Tianli	Ancient Chinese philosophical term meaning "Heavenly Principle" or "Heavenly Reason". It has profound meaning, but in the context of Xing Yi refers to natural laws, and their underlying principles. In one sense Tianli represents the "rules" of Xing Yi, that is, natural laws which cannot physically be transgressed.
Tseh	Flanking method. One of the Shen Fa.
Tseh Fa	See Tseh.
Tsi	Needles. Literally "stings".
Tsunbu	Inch Step. A Tsun (pin yin Cun) is roughly one inch. A famous stepping method in Xing Yi, which is effectively a restrained Zhong movement.
Tui	Withdraw/Drawing. One of the Shen Fa.
Tui Fa	See Tui.
Tung En Zhan	Master Ji Long Feng's military commander. An exponent of the Yue family arts.

Tuo	The Yangtze Crocodile. *Alligator sinensis.*
Tuo Xing	Character of the Crocodile.
Tushou	Barehand.
Wubing Fa	Infantry methods. The main categorisation into which Xing Yi methods fall
Wu Xin	Empty or purified spirit.
Wu Xing	Five Elements.
Wu Xing Jiaoshou	Five Elements Fighting.
Wu Xing Quan	Five Elements Boxing.
Xiao	Scabbard.
Xiaotui Fa	The coordinated application of Xing Yi in many-on-many engagements.
Xin	Spirit. Literally "heart". This is often translated as "mind", but this can be misleading. When referring to the Xin a Chinese will often point to their chest rather than their head. Xin is a dual concept in Xing Yi, in terms of the individual Xin and the Divine or Universal Xin (ideally to be unified).
Xin	Sword blade.

Xin Ding Shen Ning - Difficult to translate. Literally something like "Calm Spirit, God Better". Effectively that one may come closer to God through calming the Xin. In Xing Yi the principle of calming the Xin and removing self-centred thoughts in order to better perceive the nature of the universe.

Xin Yi   Spirit-Intention.

Xin Yu Yi He - Often translated as something like "The Xin and Yi Combine". However this neglects the word Yu which in one sense means "and", but in another can mean "gives" or "supports". Thus the Xin can also be thought of as supporting or giving rise to the Yi.

Xing   Character. Literally "shape". The essence of an animal's way of life.

Xing Yi   Character-Intention.

Xing Yi Quan - Xing Yi Boxing. A term that some people use to describe Xing Yi after the naming pattern of arts like Taiji Quan. However, for Xing Yi the -Quan part is superfluous as no other widely known usage of the combination Xing Yi exists in the Chinese language (unlike the Taiji of Taiji Quan).

Xiong   Bear.

Xiongjia   That part of the armour protecting all or part of the torso (as opposed to the limbs). The equivalent of a western breast plate or similar.

Xiong Ying   Bear-Eagle. *Spizaetus nipalensis.*

Xiong Ying He Quan - Bear and Eagle harmonised boxing.

Xiong Ying Xing - Character of the Bear Eagle.

Yan   Character of the Swallow.

Yan Xing   The direct study of wild animals for the purpose of developing a better understanding of Xing Yi.

Yanyi	Method through which a synergistic understanding of the relationship between the Yi and the Chi is developed.
Yanzi	See Yan.
Yao	Goshawk. Sometimes mis-translated as Sparrowhawk.
Yao Xing	Character of the Goshawk.
Yi	Intention.
Yi Ben	One Root. One Origin. One Nature. The fundamental basis of Xing Yi.
Yi Guan Tong Shen	- The principle of threading together the body with the Yi.
Ying	Eagle.
Ying Xing	Luo Shi - See Luo Shi.
Yingzhao	Eagle Claw.
Yi Qi	The One Chi. The energy that circulates throughout the universe.
Yi Tong	Unification. The goal of Xing Yi practice. That is unification of the practitioner with all of nature.
Yi Xin	Unified Spirit.

Yi Yu Qi He - The principle that the Yi and Chi Combine. See Xin Yu Yi He for discussion of multiple meanings of "Yu".

Yi Zi Xin Sheng - The principle that the Xin naturally gives birth to the Yi.

Yongji   A county in Shanxi Province where Ji Long Feng lived for much of his life. Its name means something like "perpetual river crossing".

Yue Chia Quan - Yue Family Boxing. Possible name of the precursor art of Xing Yi.

Yue Fei (1103-1142) - Marshal Yue Fei. The attributed founder of Xing Yi. He cannot be described as the "legendary founder", because there is indisputable evidence that he was a real person. He was martyred in 1142 and subsequently became a national hero of China.

Yue Fei Quan - Yue Fei Boxing. Possible name of the precursor art of Xing Yi.

Yundong Zai Bu - The principle that movement derives from the stepping in Xing Yi.

Zhanchang Battlefield.

Zhangu Battle drum.

Zhanju Capture/take/occupy a position of strategic importance/benefit.

Zhanmadao Large battlefield sabre.

Zhanxian The battle line. The line of integrity within a force undergoing a frontal attack.

Zhanyou Comrade(s)-in-arms.

Zhanyou Jinzuo, Zhanzuo Jinyou - The principle of simultaneous attack and defence in Xing Yi. Literally "take right, enter left; take left, enter right".

Zhatou Pierce through the space occupied by the opponent.

Zhe Hide from view/cover/screen.

Zhong Straight ahead. One of the Shen Fa.

Zhong Fa See Zhong.

Zhongnan A famous mountain associated with the early transmission of the arts that became Xing Yi.

Zhou	The elbow/forearm.
Zhua	Seize.
Zuanbu	The normal or "ordinary" way of stepping in basic Xing Yi practice (literally "Drill Step").
Zuan Jing	Drilling power. Literally the action of drilling or boring one stick into another to make fire. In Chinese Zuan has the sense of bidirectional rotation, which the English translation "Drilling" does not convey sufficiently.
Zun	Ji Long Feng's home village.
Zun Cun	See Zun.

國立故宮博物院藏品

國立故宮博物院藏品

www.ingramcontent.com/pod-product-compliance
Lightning Source LLC
LaVergne TN
LVHW081527060526
838200LV00045B/2033